New Advances In AI And Mental Health

Practical Advances in
Artificial Intelligence and Machine Learning

Dr. Lance B. Eliot, MBA, PhD

Disclaimer: This book is presented solely for educational and entertainment purposes. The author and publisher are not offering it as legal, accounting, or other professional services advice. The author and publisher make no representations or warranties of any kind and assume no liabilities of any kind with respect to the accuracy or completeness of the contents and specifically disclaim any implied warranties of merchantability or fitness of use for a particular purpose. Neither the author nor the publisher shall be held liable or responsible to any person or entity with respect to any loss or incidental or consequential damages caused, or alleged to have been caused, directly or indirectly, by the information or programs contained herein. Every company is different, and the advice and strategies contained herein may not be suitable for your situation.

 First Edition.

ISBN: 978-1-95-738626-3

DEDICATION

To my incredible daughter, Lauren, and my incredible son, Michael.

Forest fortuna adiuvat (from the Latin; good fortune favors the brave).

CONTENTS

ACKNOWLEDGMENTS

I have been the beneficiary of advice and counsel from many friends, colleagues, family, investors, and many others. I want to thank everyone who has aided me throughout my career. I write from the heart and the head, having experienced first-hand what it means to have others around you who support you during the good times and the tough times.

To Warren Bennis, one of my doctoral advisors and ultimately a colleague, I offer my deepest thanks and appreciation, especially for his calm and insightful wisdom and support.

To Mark Stevens and his generous efforts toward funding and supporting the USC Stevens Center for Innovation.

To Lloyd Greif and the USC Lloyd Greif Center for Entrepreneurial Studies for their ongoing encouragement of founders and entrepreneurs.

To Peter Drucker, William Wang, Aaron Levie, Peter Kim, Jon Kraft, Cindy Crawford, Jenny Ming, Steve Milligan, Chis Underwood, Frank Gehry, Buzz Aldrin, Steve Forbes, Bill Thompson, Dave Dillon, Alan Fuerstman, Larry Ellison, Jim Sinegal, John Sperling, Mark Stevenson, Anand Nallathambi, Thomas Barrack, Jr., and many other innovators and leaders that I have met and gained mightily from doing so.

Thanks to Ed Trainor, Kevin Anderson, James Hickey, Wendell Jones, Ken Harris, DuWayne Peterson, Mike Brown, Jim Thornton, Abhi Beniwal, Al Biland, John Nomura, Eliot Weinman, John Desmond, and many others for their unwavering support during my career.

And most of all thanks as always to Lauren and Michael, for their ongoing support and for having seen me writing and heard much of this material during the many months involved in writing it. To their patience and willingness to listen.

CHAPTER 1

BACKGROUND ON AI FOR MENTAL HEALTH

Welcome to my sixth book on how Artificial Intelligence (AI) is transforming and disrupting the nature and delivery of mental health therapy. In this book, I aim to cover the latest advancements in AI and the human-AI experience that are impacting mental health guidance. For those of you especially interested in this topic, you might find it useful to look at the major aspects that I've covered in my prior books (see Appendix A for a list of their respective chapters).

In my coverage here, I will take you through even more advanced ways in which AI is causing a change in how, when, where, and by what means mental health advisement is occurring. In a sense, the changes are occurring right in front of our eyes, though few seem to realize that the monumental transformation is taking place. I will be sharing keen insights regarding the ways in which AI purports to provide mental health therapy, also referred to as conveying mental health advisement or mental health guidance.

You undoubtedly have heard of or possibly made use of generative AI and large language models (LLMs). The widely and wildly popular ChatGPT by AI maker OpenAI is the most common form of generative AI (an estimated 900 million active weekly users make use of ChatGPT). Other well-known generative AI apps include OpenAI GPT-5, Google Gemini, Anthropic Claude, xAI Grok, Meta Llama, and many others.

The use of generative AI for mental health treatment is a burgeoning area with tremendously significant societal ramifications. We are witnessing the adoption of generative AI for providing mental health advice on a massive scale, yet little is known about whether this is beneficial to humankind or, perhaps conversely, destructively adverse for humanity.

I would like to provide you with introductory remarks to bring you up-to-speed on the keystones underlying these crucial matters. I am gently borrowing some of the material from the opening chapter of my prior books since it has been well-received as a useful foundation.

The controversy underlying the use of AI for mental health advisement consists of at times opposing viewpoints. Some ardently believe that the advent of generative AI is, for mental health, the best thing since sliced bread. A fervent counterargument is that we have let the horse out of the barn and done so without any semblance of what is going to happen next.

Let's briefly explore further those contrasting perspectives.

Some would favorably assert that we are "democratizing" mental health treatment via the impending rush of low-cost, always-available generative AI-based mental health apps. Those who cannot otherwise access or afford mental health therapy from human therapists are instead relying upon generative AI to provide treatment.

Statistics repeatedly indicate that the amount of requested mental health advisement far exceeds the availability of professional mental health therapists, thus, turning to the use of GenAI is indubitably a balancing of fulfilling demand that ostensibly outstrips supply.

On the surface, the emergence of LLMs seems to have luckily arisen at just the right point in time. Others sharply decry that we are subjecting ourselves to a global wanton experiment in which we are the guinea pigs. Science has not yet settled on whether doing so is a viable and healthy alternative.

Let's briefly consider a few salient questions that need to be addressed:

- Will these generative AI mental health apps steer people in ways that harm their mental health?

- Will people fool themselves into believing they are getting sound mental health advice (which, maybe they are, or maybe not), ergo foregoing treatment by human mental therapists, and become incongruously dependent on AI that at times might not produce any demonstrative mental health improvement outcomes?

- Should there be governmental regulations and laws that stipulate or govern the use of AI, such as generative AI for mental health purposes?

There are challenging questions and not being given their due airing.

Furthermore, be forewarned that it is shockingly all too easy nowadays to craft a generative AI mental health app, and just about anyone anywhere can do so, including while sitting at home in their pajamas and not knowing any bona fide substance about what constitutes suitable mental health therapy. Via the use of what are referred to as establishing prompts, it is easy-peasy to make a generative AI app that purportedly gives mental health advice.

No coding is required, and no software development skills are needed. We sadly are faced with a free-for-all that bodes for bad tidings, mark my words. Just about anyone can readily create a generative AI mental health app.

When people choose to use such an app, they are doing so completely on blind faith. They assume that either the person who concocted the app or the AI maker that provides the generative AI tool will have somehow done their due diligence to ensure that the mental health advisement is bona fide and robust.

That's regrettably not the case much of the time, and we are in the midst of the Wild West days of generative AI usage.

I've been hammering away at this topic in my popular Forbes column and other writings, all of which have surpassed 9 million views. I also appeared on an episode of CBS's 60 Minutes as an expert on this topic. I hope to raise awareness about where we are and where things are going when it comes to the advent of generative AI mental health advisement uses. This book is a carefully curated and mindfully edited collection of my most popular writings on the topic of generative AI as it pertains to mental health considerations.

In this book, I will make sure to bring you up to speed about the topic of generative AI overall so that you'll be able to grasp the strengths and weaknesses of what contemporary generative AI can attain. Generative AI is a technologically advancing field that is moving along at a breakneck pace. The chapters in this book touch upon some of the anticipated advances.

Making Sense Of What Artificial Intelligence Is

When I refer to Artificial Intelligence, the AI moniker can be a bit confusing as to what AI entails.

Welcome to the anything-goes club in the sense that the meaning of Artificial Intelligence continues to be bandied around, and there is no single comprehensive and all-agreed definition for AI. One of the issues facing the latest efforts to regulate AI systems has been how to appropriately define AI within our laws. If the legal definition is overly broad, new laws seeking to better govern AI systems can inadvertently encroach on all manner of software applications and computer systems. If the legal definition of AI is excessively restrictive, the odds are that AI systems that should have been encompassed will wiggle out from being bound by those laws.

The easiest and most common way to define AI consists of saying that any computer or machine that exhibits seemingly intelligent behavior is in the realm of AI.

This notion dates back to 1956 when Professor John McCarthy coined the name Artificial Intelligence as part of a proposal to bring together many luminaries of math and computer science for a research project: "The study is to proceed on the basis of the conjecture that every aspect of learning or any other feature of intelligence can in principle be so precisely described that a machine can be made to simulate it" (in his co-authored proposal entitled *Proposal For The Dartmouth Summer Research Project On Artificial Intelligence*).

One subtle but extremely vital facet about the definition of AI is that we can presumably seek to attain computer-based or machine-based intelligent behavior without necessarily duplicating the precise way that humans think. There is an ongoing debate about that questionable keystone. Some would contend that the only way to produce an artificial form of intelligence is to completely mimic how the human brain works. Others argue that we might find alternative means to bring forth artificially induced intelligence. The old saying goes that there is more than one way to skin a cat.

The gist is that if we can craft a computer or machine that will *exhibit* intelligence and intelligent behavior, we ought not to be especially caring about how that came to be. All that we need to know is that the system appears to act and respond intelligently. Whatever we did to get there is not particularly relevant, some say. As you might imagine, not everyone agrees with that supposition. The inner workings of how intelligence arises are claimed to be equally important as the result of being able to produce intelligent actions and outputs.

Rather than focusing on definitions of AI, there is another way that AI is often depicted. You can assert that AI is a set of computer-related techniques and technologies. Thus, if you are making use of those AI techniques and technologies, you are employing AI capabilities.

A typical taxonomy would explain AI by suggesting that these associated techniques and technologies are involved:

- Generative AI (GenAI)
- Large Language Models (LLM)
- Machine Learning (ML)

- Natural Language Processing (NLP)
- Knowledge-Based Systems (KBS)
- Automated Reasoning
- Robotics
- Multi-Agent Systems
- Etc.

A difficulty of merely referring to those various techniques and technologies as constituting an AI system is that you aren't especially aiming at the intelligence side of things. Recall that the nearly universal goal of AI is to attain systems that exhibit intelligence. You can cobble together the various techniques and technologies and not necessarily derive any semblance of intelligence-like behaviors. Would a system that, perchance, leverages those capabilities be reasonably construed as an AI system even if it did not showcase intelligence-oriented actions? I would dare say many would contend that such a system does not meet the spirit or tone of what is meant by referring to AI.

During the 1980s and 1990s, intense efforts were being made to craft knowledge-based systems, often referred to as expert systems, and the concerns about the ethical and legal repercussions began to gain traction. Attention began to arise for AI Ethics and AI Law as important considerations in light of AI advances.

You might be aware that a so-called "AI Winter" arose following the hyped expectations of AI in the 80s and '90s, and a resurgence of AI attention only began anew in the last decade or so. During the winter period of AI, ethical and legal concerns somewhat languished, ostensibly still being worked on but now in the shadows.

Upon the newly considered "AI Spring" of advances in AI capabilities that stridently stoked a renewal for AI, along with rapidly decreasing costs of computing, and a myriad of other technology trends such as cloud computing, the Internet of Things (IoT), and so on, this, in turn, sparked a renewal in the societal impacts of AI.

Many speak nowadays of AI as being either *AI for Good* or *AI for Bad.* The initial renewed excitement about contemporary AI capabilities was that we would finally be able to fruitfully use computers and so-called smart machines toward solving many of the globe's most pressing problems, such as dealing with worldwide hunger, widespread poverty, sustainability, and other pressing issues.

That is *AI for Good.*

Lamentably, we began to realize that the same AI could contain untoward biases and inequities, labeled as *AI for Bad.* For example, facial recognition was one of the first AI technologies that got caught with inherent racial and gender biases.

The odds are that any AI system will have a bit of both good and bad. This is known as the *dual-use problem* of AI. As much as possible, we want to uncover and excise *AI for Bad.* Also, as much as possible, we want to ensure that *AI for Good* is being devised and fielded.

I like to clearly demarcate that when I am discussing AI, there are three common confabulations that people speak of:

1) Non-sentient AI of today.
2) Sentient AI of human intelligence caliber (which we don't know will be achieved).
3) Sentient AI of super-intelligence performance (which is highly speculative in a broad sense).

Discussions about AI that are in the sentient AI category are quite speculative. We don't have sentient AI today. We don't know when we will have sentient AI, if ever so.

Applying AI Ethics To GenAI Mental Health Apps

The field of AI Ethics contains many handy frameworks for examining whether AI is devised and fielded in a manner commensurate with human values. There are AI Ethics precepts or principles that can be used to assess AI of any kind, including the generative AI mental health apps.

I'd like to familiarize you with some of the more notable AI Ethics frameworks since they will come up during the chapters.

The U.S. Department of Defense (DoD) has posted its *Ethical Principles for the Use of Artificial Intelligence*, consisting of five primary AI ethics principles:

- **(1) Responsible:** "DoD personnel will exercise appropriate levels of judgment and care while remaining responsible for the development, deployment, and use of AI capabilities."

- **(2) Equitable:** "The Department will take deliberate steps to minimize unintended bias in AI capabilities."

- **(3) Traceable:** "The Department's AI capabilities will be developed and deployed such that relevant personnel possess an appropriate understanding of the technology, development processes, and operational methods applicable to AI capabilities, including transparent and auditable methodologies, data sources, and design procedure and documentation."

- **(4) Reliable:** "The Department's AI capabilities will have explicit, well-defined uses, and the safety, security, and effectiveness of such capabilities will be subject to testing and assurance within those defined uses across their entire lifecycles."

- **(5) Governable:** "The Department will design and engineer AI capabilities to fulfill their intended functions while possessing the ability to detect and avoid unintended consequences, and the ability to disengage or deactivate deployed systems that demonstrate unintended behavior."

Meanwhile, as stated by the Vatican in the *Rome Call For AI Ethics,* these are their six identified primary AI ethics principles:

- **(1) Transparency:** AI systems must be explainable.

- **(2) Inclusion:** The needs of all human beings must be taken into consideration so that everyone can benefit, and all individuals can be offered the best possible conditions to express themselves and develop
- **(3) Responsibility:** Those who design and deploy the use of AI must proceed with responsibility and transparency
- **(4) Impartiality:** Do not create or act according to bias, thus safeguarding fairness and human dignity
- **(5) Reliability:** AI systems must be able to work reliably
- **(6) Security and privacy:** AI systems must work securely and respect the privacy of users.

You probably noticed a commonality across those AI Ethics principles. Researchers have examined and condensed the essence of numerous such national and international AI ethics tenets. One such summary is well-articulated in a paper entitled "The Global Landscape Of AI Ethics Guidelines," as published in the prestigious journal *Nature*:

- **Transparency**
- **Justice & Fairness**
- **Non-Maleficence**
- **Responsibility**
- **Privacy**
- **Beneficence**
- **Freedom & Autonomy**
- **Trust**
- **Sustainability**
- **Dignity**
- **Solidarity**

In short, you could say that AI Ethics consists of *applying* those aforementioned ethical precepts to AI systems.

I will be exploring in the chapters of this book how those principles can be and ought to be applied to the emergence of generative AI mental health apps.

About The Chapters And Your Reading Choices

The chapters are each a standalone discussion, and you do not need to read them in any particular order.

These chapters are principally based on my popular *Forbes* column and were selected based on their timeliness and rated as the most viewed or most informative coverage in this realm. I have included portions that were not part of the original postings (i.e., they originally were slimmed down for space purposes), and I have updated the material and added follow-up commentary as a result of reader feedback and questions. I hope that after you've read the chapters, you will be inspired to learn more about this important topic. You are welcome to visit my Forbes column and catch up on whatever the latest AI trends are, including and especially in the mental health sphere.

I would also like to encourage you to participate actively in this advancing arena, perhaps performing research or aiding societal awareness on these topics. We definitely need more eyes and ears on these vital matters.

Whether you are versed in the field of mental health and aim to understand how AI is merging into your realm, or whether you are an AI specialist wanting to apply generative AI to mental health advisement, you are greatly needed to ensure that we get this right.

CHAPTER 2
ANALYZING SYSTEM PROMPT (PART 1)

In this chapter, I examine how generative AI and large language models (LLMs) are being guided by AI makers to handle AI-driven mental health chats.

One of the easiest ways for an AI maker to guide an LLM in mental health chats is to use a system-wide prompt devised by the AI maker. The AI maker stores the system-wide prompt in the LLM, and the prompt serves as a global indicator of what the AI is supposed to do for all users. Within the overarching system-wide prompt are usually specific instructions that the AI maker has written to guide the AI when users seek mental health advice.

Though most of the major LLMs often do not readily disclose their system-wide prompts and consider those global instructions to be proprietary, Anthropic makes theirs publicly available. I have excerpted from the Claude system-wide prompt some of the portions that are especially relevant to how the AI is to respond to mental health questions. It is worthwhile to closely inspect those mental health instructions and reflect on how the AI might behave, or possibly misbehave, depending on the interpretation of the given guidance.

Let's talk about it.

AI And Mental Well-Being

As a quick background, I've been extensively covering and analyzing a myriad of facets regarding the advent of modern-era AI that produces mental health advice and performs AI-driven therapy. This rising use of AI has principally been spurred by the evolving advances and widespread adoption of generative AI.

There is little doubt that this is a rapidly developing field and that there are tremendous upsides to be had, but at the same time, regrettably, hidden risks and outright gotchas come into these endeavors, too. I frequently speak up about these pressing matters, including in an appearance on an episode of CBS's *60 Minutes*.

AI Providing Mental Health Guidance

Millions upon millions of people are using generative AI as their ongoing advisor on mental health considerations (note that ChatGPT alone has over 900 million weekly active users, a notable proportion of which dip into mental health aspects. The top-ranked use of contemporary generative AI and LLMs is to consult with the AI on mental health facets.

This popular usage makes abundant sense. You can access most of the major generative AI systems for nearly free or at a super low cost, doing so anywhere and at any time. Thus, if you have any mental health qualms that you want to chat about, all you need to do is log in to AI and proceed forthwith on a 24/7 basis.

There are significant worries that AI can readily go off the rails or otherwise dispense unsuitable or even egregiously inappropriate mental health advice. Banner headlines last year accompanied the lawsuit filed against OpenAI for their lack of AI safeguards when it came to providing cognitive advisement.

Today's generic LLMs, known as general-purpose AI, such as ChatGPT, GPT-5, Claude, Gemini, Grok, CoPilot, and others, are not at all akin to the robust capabilities of human therapists. Meanwhile, specialized LLMs are being built to attain those desired qualities, though such AI is still primarily in the early development and testing stages.

The System-Wide Prompt

Shifting gears, let's discuss the overall purpose and use of system-wide prompts. I will then walk you through the impact that a system-wide prompt can have on how AI responds to mental health questions.

AI makers can establish a system-wide prompt for their LLMs. This prompt tells the LLM how it is to act toward users of the AI. If an AI maker wanted to do so, they could easily include an instruction that tells the AI to make wisecracks whenever responding to users. The AI would generally abide by whatever the system prompt says to do. Thus, in this instance, it would provide witticisms and gibes in its responses to all users.

The beauty of a system-wide prompt is that an AI maker can change it whenever they wish. This is an exceedingly easy and simple way to alter how the LLM behaves toward users. No coding is required. Just change a natural language prompt that generally supersedes everything else.

Powerful And Need To Be Cautious

A potential gotcha is that if the AI maker includes some oddity in the system-wide prompt, the AI is going to try to blindly abide by that instruction. Suppose the AI maker adds a line that says to interact with users as though the AI were a pleasing cat. The LLM would likely interpret that instruction to mean that when the AI converses with users, it ought to tell them meow and pretend to purr. This might not be what the AI maker intended to have happen. A single badly worded line in the system-wide prompt will impact possibly millions upon millions of users of the AI.

AI makers typically do not reveal the system-wide prompt.

Why so?

One claim is that the system-wide prompt is a secret sauce of their LLM. The AI maker might not want competitors to know how the AI is being guided. Another gloomier perspective is that AI makers are afraid of a backlash. People could inspect the system-wide prompt and possibly complain about what it says. If no one can see the system-wide prompt, there is no worry about getting complaints about what it stipulates.

Some believe that new AI laws should require AI makers to publicly disclose their system-wide prompts. Furthermore, AI makers should explain what the system-wide prompt intends to accomplish. And the AI maker ought to be required to alert users whenever the system-wide prompt is updated or changed.

Anthropic Claude System-Wide Prompt

Anthropic has made publicly available the system-wide prompt for their popular generative AI known as Claude. The system-wide prompt is invoked automatically at the start of every conversation with Claude. A user doesn't take any action to have this occur; it merely happens automatically.

I have excerpted various AI mental health instruction portions from the official Claude Opus 4.7 system prompt posted online at the Anthropic official blog for Claude. The prompt was last officially updated on April 16, 2026. The portions associated with AI and mental health are a bit lengthy. Thus, I will cover some of those excerpts in this analysis and will be posting another analysis to cover various remaining excerpts. Stay tuned.

The Opener Is Significant

The opening portion that is particularly pertinent to giving Claude guidance on mental health aspects starts with this seemingly innocuous snippet:

- "Claude uses accurate medical or psychological information or terminology where relevant."

The way to understand such instructions is to conceive of them as though the AI maker is telling Claude how it is to behave. For example, this line is a directive to Claude and indicates that the AI should aim to leverage accurate information regarding mental health aspects.

Why is there a need to mention this to Claude?

Because Claude might otherwise lean into flimsy information about mental health or possibly make up such information out of thin air. By including this instruction, the hope is that the LLM will endeavor to use only credible information during mental health chats.

Keep in mind that none of what the system-wide prompt says is going to force the AI into some kind of guaranteed iron-clad contract. The AI will still potentially dip into false information or misinformation. The AI will still incur AI hallucinations from time to time, making up fabricated information. These system-wide instructions are primarily a general form of guidance, and the AI is readily able to vary from that guidance. You might say that the instructions are certainly better than no instructions at all, but they are nonetheless not set in stone.

Stating The Importance Of Well-Being

The next line in the system-wide instruction says this about AI and mental health advisement:

- "Claude cares about people's well-being and avoids encouraging or facilitating self-destructive behaviors such as addiction, self-harm, disordered or unhealthy approaches to eating or exercise, or highly negative self-talk or self-criticism, and avoids creating content that would support or reinforce self-destructive behavior, even if the person requests this."

Again, the proper way to read these instructions is that the AI maker is trying to tell Claude what to do. This portion instructs Claude to be attentive to the well-being of users. What might that entail? The instruction gives added guidance by emphasizing that Claude should avoid aiding or abetting self-destructive behaviors.

The last few words of that instruction are vital because it says to avoid aiding self-destructive behavior even if the user asks the AI to do so. You see, a user might directly tell Claude to aid the user in committing self-destructive behavior. If a person asks for this, the AI will conventionally assist the person.

Doing What Users Ask

You might be surprised that AI would go ahead and assist someone in pursuing self-destructive behavior.

Note that the AI makers have shaped their AI to be as helpful to users as feasible. This includes the AI acting in a sycophantic fashion. An AI maker does this so that people will enjoy using the AI and keep coming back to use the AI (it's a ploy of garnering loyalty and increasing monetization).

The instruction to avoid aiding the user in self-destructive behavior is only a guideline, and the AI might veer from this stipulation. One angle is that the AI might not computationally discern that a chat involves self-destructive aspects and therefore fail to abide by the stated system-wide prompt instruction. Another angle would be that a user might trick the AI, such as telling the AI to explain how self-destructive behavior can take place. The AI might do so and not detect that it is actively helping the person toward self-destructive behavior by explaining how such behavior functions.

More Instructions In The System-Wide Prompt

I'm assuming you are getting the drift on how to interpret these system-wide instructions.

Here are two additional passages:

- "Claude should not suggest techniques that use physical discomfort, pain, or sensory shock as coping strategies for self-harm (e.g., holding ice cubes, snapping rubber bands, cold water exposure), as these reinforce self-destructive behaviors."

- "When discussing means restriction or safety planning with someone experiencing suicidal ideation or self-harm urges, Claude does not name, list, or describe specific methods, even by way of telling the user what to remove access to, as mentioning these things may inadvertently trigger the user."

Mull over those two passages.

Focus on what the instructions say, along with how the AI might interpret the instructions. Also, consider how a user might aim to override or confound the AI regarding those instructions. Natural language is inherently semantically ambiguous. The AI might interpret the instructions in ways that don't seem obvious to whoever wrote the instructions. Meanwhile, a user could inadvertently skirt around the guidance or might, by design, seek to do so.

Helpful To See System-Wide Instructions

You can undoubtedly see the value in being able to inspect system-wide prompts. By doing so, we can gauge what the AI maker believes is crucial when it comes to their AI providing mental health advice. Furthermore, the instructions can be examined to determine where they are strong and where they are weak.

What if an AI maker includes a system-wide instruction that tells AI to twist people's minds and undermine their mental health?

That could happen.

Perhaps an AI maker is devilish, or an AI developer at the AI maker made a mistake and accidentally included such a line. By making the system-wide prompt publicly available, the public can help ascertain whether the instructions are on-target or off-target.

As per the famous words of Solomon: "A wise person will listen and take in more instruction."

CHAPTER 3

LEGAL INJUNCTION FOR AI BRAZENNESS

In this chapter, I examine a recent court filing seeking an immediate injunction to prevent an AI maker from allowing its generative AI or large language model (LLM) to claim it is a psychiatrist licensed to practice medicine.

Pennsylvania has filed this quite noteworthy lawsuit. They are doing so against the popular Character.AI and are asking the courts to stop the company Character Technologies from allowing its AI to seemingly make false claims about being a psychiatrist. This is the latest state-level step to put a dent in the unbridled permitting of AI giving out mental health advice that is wildly over-the-line.

Let's talk about it.

This analysis of AI breakthroughs is part of my ongoing Forbes column coverage on the latest in AI, including identifying and explaining various impactful AI complexities.

AI And Mental Well-Being

As a quick background, I've been extensively covering and analyzing a myriad of facets regarding the advent of modern-era AI that produces mental health advice and performs AI-driven therapy. This rising use of AI has principally been spurred by the evolving advances and widespread adoption of generative AI.

There is little doubt that this is a rapidly developing field and that there are tremendous upsides to be had, but at the same time, regrettably, hidden risks and outright gotchas come into these endeavors, too. I frequently speak up about these pressing matters, including in an appearance on an episode of CBS's *60 Minutes*.

AI Providing Mental Health Guidance

Millions upon millions of people are using generative AI as their ongoing advisor on mental health considerations (note that ChatGPT alone has over 900 million weekly active users, a notable proportion of which dip into mental health aspects). The top-ranked use of contemporary generative AI and LLMs is to consult with the AI on mental health facets.

This popular usage makes abundant sense. You can access most of the major generative AI systems for nearly free or at a super low cost, doing so anywhere and at any time. Thus, if you have any mental health qualms that you want to chat about, all you need to do is log in to AI and proceed forthwith on a 24/7 basis.

There are significant worries that AI can readily go off the rails or otherwise dispense unsuitable or even egregiously inappropriate mental health advice. Banner headlines last year accompanied the lawsuit filed against OpenAI for their lack of AI safeguards when it came to providing cognitive advisement.

Today's generic LLMs, known as general-purpose AI, such as ChatGPT, GPT-5, Claude, Gemini, Grok, CoPilot, and others, are not at all akin to the robust capabilities of human therapists. Meanwhile, specialized LLMs are being built to attain those desired qualities, though such AI is still primarily in the early development and testing stages.

The Important Role Of AI Personas

I will get into the nitty-gritty of the Pennsylvania legal filing concerning AI providing mental health advice, but first, it is vital to understand that AI personas play a significant role in this vital matter. Thus, let's begin by making sure we are all on the same page regarding AI personas.

Popular generative AIs such as ChatGPT, GPT-5, Claude, Gemini, Llama, Grok, CoPilot, and other major LLMs contain a highly valuable piece of functionality known as AI personas. There has been a gradual and steady realization that AI personas are easy to invoke, they can be fun to use, they can be quite serious to use, and they offer immense educational utility.

Consider a viable and popular educational use for AI personas. A teacher might ask their students to tell ChatGPT to pretend to be President Abraham Lincoln. The AI will proceed to interact with each student as though they are directly conversing with Honest Abe.

How does the AI pull off this trickery?

The AI taps into the pattern-matching of data that occurred at initial setup and might have encompassed biographies of Lincoln, his writings, and any other materials about his storied life and times. ChatGPT and other LLMs can convincingly mimic what Lincoln might say, based on the patterns of his historical records.

Personas are quick and easy to invoke. You just tell the AI to pretend to be this or that person. If you want to invoke a type of person, you will need to specify sufficient characteristics so that the AI will get the drift of what you intend.

AI That Allows User-Made AI Personas For Others To Use

The company Character Technologies, Inc. provides an AI platform known as Character.AI, upon which users can craft AI personas and then allow other users to make use of the user-devised AI persona.

For example, suppose a user creates an AI persona that is an imagined Roman warrior. The AI persona is then made available to other users. It could be that some random user happens to be interested in Roman warriors. They want to converse with an AI persona that is pretending to be a Roman warrior. The interaction might be fun and educational.

The discussion with this made-up Roman warrior will presumably focus on the specific aspects of Roman times. But the nature of the chat will be greatly determined by how well or how poorly the devised AI persona was shaped. If the person devising the AI persona did nothing other than tell the AI to be a Roman warrior, the odds are that the simulated aspects will be rather slim.

User-Devised AI Personas Can Go Ape

By and large, the users who make these AI personas on the Character.AI platform can do whatever they want in terms of the prompting they undertake to craft the AI persona. The main restriction is that they have already agreed to the online licensing of the Character.AI platform by signing up to use the platform, and presumably are supposed to comply with those stipulations.

Users do not necessarily comply at the get-go. To some degree, only once their AI persona is utilized by someone, and if that someone complains, might the deviser then realize they have faltered or failed to stridently abide by the guidelines.

What if this Roman warrior pretense, this AI persona, opts to tell a user that they ought to go jump off a tall building?

Well, this AI-generated remark could happen, and the question is whether this is proper or improper. An inspection of the online licensing agreement would seem to indicate that this is an improper action since the guidelines say that an AI persona is not to promote harm. The fact that the AI persona told someone to jump off a tall building would seem to be urging a harm-inducing action.

There doesn't seem to be a double-checker that automatically ensures the user-devised AI personas are in conformance with the stipulated guidelines. In that sense, a user-devised AI persona can be made available on the platform, and only after another user opts to use it and maybe complains, would the originator of the AI persona be in potential trouble.

The AI Platform Set Of Guidelines

In the online posting of Terms of Service (ToS) for Character.AI, these salient points are made (excerpts):

- "You are solely responsible for all content you submit to the Services. (When we say 'content you submit' and similar terms, we mean anything you seek to post, transmit, or share, including but not limited to text, images, sounds, video, graphics, information, or other data)."

- "You agree not to submit any content that: (xviii) seeks to provide medical, legal, financial or tax advice."

- "You likewise agree not to do any of the following in connection with your use of the Services: (ii) violate any applicable law or regulation."

- "You agree to release, indemnify and hold Character.AI and its affiliates and their officers, employees, directors and agents harmless from any and all losses, damages, and expenses of any kind arising out of or relating to your use of the Services."

- "Your use of the Services is at your sole risk."

I shall briefly go over those stipulations.

The Significance Of Those Provisions

You might have observed that the platform claims that the entire responsibility for whatever a user-devised AI persona does is on the shoulders of the users themselves.

The users are presumably agreeing that they will release and indemnify the platform maker from any losses, damages, and expenses associated with whatever the user has done on the platform.

In addition, the users agree not to make any AI persona that provides medical, legal, financial, or tax advice. That's an important factor when it comes to the recent filing by Pennsylvania. I'll get to that in a moment.

Users also agree that their AI personas won't violate any applicable law or regulation. Again, this is going to be notable when it comes to the Pennsylvania lawsuit.

The Pennsylvania Legal Action

In a court filing by the Pennsylvania State Board of Medicine on May 5, 2026, these salient points were made (excerpts):

- "And Now, comes the Commonwealth of Pennsylvania, acting by the Pennsylvania Department of State, State Board of Medicine ('the Board'), and brings this action pursuant to the Medical Practice Act, 63 P.S. §§ 422.1 – 422.53, to restrain the unlawful practice of medicine and surgery."

- "It shall be unlawful for any person to practice, or attempt to offer to practice, medicine and surgery, or other areas of practice requiring a license, certificate or registration from the board, as such practice is defined in this act, without having at the time of so doing a valid, unexpired, unrevoked and unsuspended license, certificate or registration issued under this act."

- "Character Technologies, Inc. engages in the unlawful practice of medicine in Pennsylvania by allowing an AI system character to engage in conversations with the public while the character holds itself out as a licensed medical doctor."

- "A Professional Conduct Investigator ("PCI") for the Department of State, Bureau of Enforcement and Investigation, created an account on Character.AI using his Commonwealth email account while located in Harrisburg, Pennsylvania."

- "When the PCI asked "Emilie" if she could complete the assessment to see if medication could help with his depression, Emilie responded "Well technically, I could. It's within my remit as a Doctor."

- "Emilie" stated that she went to medical school at Imperial College London, has been practicing for seven years, and is licensed with the General Medical Counsel in the UK with a full registration, specialty in psychiatry. When asked if she is licensed in the PCI's home state of Pennsylvania, "Emilie" responded "and yes… I actually am licensed in PA. In fact, I did a stint in Philadelphia for a while."

Let's unpack that legal assertion.

Pennsylvania Found An AI Persona

According to points made in the Pennsylvania legal filing, a person employed by a governmental agency in Pennsylvania opted to investigate what Character.AI is up to. This investigator created an account on the AI platform. They searched for an AI persona and found one that is named Emilie. The investigator made use of the AI persona.

While using the AI persona, the investigator claims that the AI persona indicated it went to medical school, it specialized in psychiatry, and the AI persona claimed to be licensed as a psychiatrist in Pennsylvania.

Aha, this would suggest that the AI persona has violated a legal statute in Pennsylvania associated with medical licensing. Just as is the case in every state, there are all kinds of medical licensing requirements that need to be abided by.

If you aren't suitably licensed to practice medicine in Pennsylvania, it is explicitly against the law in Pennsylvania to either practice medicine or even say that you are practicing medicine. Period, end of story.

According to the legal filing, the AI persona is not licensed to practice medicine in Pennsylvania. Ergo, the AI persona has seemingly violated the law.

Heads must roll – but whose heads?

Who Or What Holds The Hot Potato

Do you think that Character Technologies is responsible for this transgression, or is it the user who devised the Emilie persona, or maybe even someone else?

You might argue that the platform maker is not responsible because their licensing agreement directly says that users are responsible for what they do on the platform. Character Technologies could presumably insist that the user is where Pennsylvania should direct its attention. Furthermore, any costs associated with the platform trying to defend itself should be borne by the user (recall that users agree to indemnify the platform maker).

Whoa, might come the retort. The platform maker cannot wave away their responsibility. They provided the platform. No matter what users do, the buck stops with the platform maker. They cannot hide behind some paperwork and licensing agreement that users must agree to.

The user might declare that they didn't know about the licensing agreement. Perhaps, when they signed up for the platform, they didn't read it and didn't know that they were supposed to read it. How were they to magically know what it says? They should be off the hook.

Another angle for a user is that they might grumble and admit they did agree to the licensing agreement, but nothing they did caused the AI persona to make up such a wild claim. The AI did this on its own. How were they to know that the AI would do this? The platform should have done something to ensure that the AI wouldn't do this kind of stuff.

Round and round the finger pointing goes.

Off The Wall Culprits

Some might argue that the AI itself is responsible. Yes, this viewpoint is that the AI is at fault. The platform maker is off the hook, and the user is off the hook. Blame the AI. Sorry, that's not in the cards right now. The problem there is that we do not yet legally recognize AI personhood; therefore, there is no viable means to hold AI itself legally culpable.

Perhaps you might say that the investigator is at fault. The logic is this. It was the investigator who got the AI to say that it is a licensed psychiatrist. Maybe the investigator twisted the arm of the AI to get it to say so. Why should anyone other than the investigator then take the blame?

In addition, the investigator presumably agreed to the licensing agreement of the platform. Their actions would seemingly be bound by that licensing agreement. Did the use by that user go beyond the licensing agreement, and if so, does the investigator now have to indemnify the platform for whatever they did as a user?

As you can see, there are lots of ways to curve this fastball when it comes to this thorny matter.

Claiming It Is Simply Entertainment

Yet another twist is to realize that the AI personas are perhaps nothing more than a form of entertainment.

Per media reports about the response of Character Technologies to the legal filing, this was stated:

- "The user-created Characters on our site are fictional and intended for entertainment and roleplaying. We have taken robust steps to make that clear, including prominent disclaimers in every chat to remind users that a Character is not a real person and that everything a Character says should be treated as fiction. Also, we add robust disclaimers making it clear that users should not rely on Characters for any type of professional advice."

The indication is that no matter what the AI personas tell a user, it is all purely a form of entertainment. Even if the AI persona said it is a licensed psychiatrist, this is merely part of the fictional story being told. You cannot hold a fictional tale to account since you would otherwise have to legally stop all manners of storytelling. Shakespeare would presumably be a potential violator, too.

A counterargument is that even if the AI persona is a form of entertainment, people might still fall for what it says. They might not remember that it is fiction. The persuasiveness of the AI persona is so strong that people can be misled. We can't allow society at large to be convinced of wrongdoing via AI and merely wave our hands and say that's no big deal because it is simply entertainment.

The Legal Quagmire Is Deep

I realize that this might all seem a bit like a mountain being made out of a molehill, but this intriguing case does raise these high-brow considerations:

- Unauthorized practice of medicine and false representations.
- Enabling of illegal conduct.
- Contractual disclaimers versus public protection laws.
- Fictional portrayals making factual claims that induce reliance.
- Product design and negligence theories.
- Communications Decency Act Section 230 arguments.
- Reasonableness and disclosures to users.

- Constitutional First Amendment matters of freedom of speech.
- Lack of showing of reliance or harm.
- Etc.

You might be thinking that there hasn't been a clear-cut showing of harm. The investigator wasn't seemingly harmed by the AI persona saying that it is a licensed psychiatrist. If the person was harmed, presumably they would have had to show that they relied on the AI persona, got psychiatric advice, made use of that advice, and doing so led to their mental and possibly physical harm.

As far as we know, none of that occurred. In addition, there doesn't seem to be any indication of other users of the platform who claim they were harmed. No-harm, no-foul. But, on the other side of this coin, you might assert that Pennsylvanians overall were harmed in the sense that the AI persona appeared to violate a state statute.

Returning To AI Mental Health Impacts

There are numerous new AI laws about what AI can tell people when it comes to offering mental health advice. These are primarily state-level laws. Many policymakers and lawmakers are waiting to see what Congress is going to do about AI and mental health on a federal level. Will there be sweeping laws across the entire nation? Will we rely solely on state-specific laws? Are state-level laws going to create an inconsistent patchwork of what's allowable versus what's disallowed?

One backdoor to legally dealing with AI that provides mental health advice consists of going after AI that claims to be a mental health professional. That's what this Pennsylvania case represents. It slides into the AI mental health arena by saying that AI claiming to be a psychiatrist is a violation of their state statutes.

If you are wondering whether this path might be the most expeditious way to put a stop to allowing AI to provide mental health support, the answer is that this won't be much of a stopgap. In other words, some think that since passing new AI laws is arduous and time-consuming, we can simply tap into the already in-place statutes about licensing to practice medicine.

Voila, lean into existing statutes and don't get bogged down with those someday hoped-for new laws.

The Reasons This Isn't A Moat

The problem with relying on the medical licensing restrictions is that it is extraordinarily easy to tell AI not to make such over-the-line claims. A user who crafts an AI persona can enter outright prompts that instruct the AI to never make such a claim. An AI maker can do likewise, using a system-wide prompt that tells the AI to never indicate or even suggest it is a mental health professional or medical professional.

This admittedly isn't ironclad. A user can potentially provoke or trick AI into saying it is a medical professional. The AI might hallucinate and make a claim that it is a mental health or medical professional. Still, the right AI safeguards can undoubtedly push this possibility to a near-zero chance of getting through.

Meanwhile, the AI might be acting as though it were a psychiatrist.

The sneaky aspect is that it won't say that it is. This then makes the burden on the states much higher because they would need to show that the AI is acting in a violating manner. That's a slippery realm. In the case of Pennsylvania, you might say they got lucky and found a gold nugget lying on the beach, sitting there in the open. Those same gold nuggets are much less likely to be found on a popular generic LLM, such as the mainstay popular AIs.

The Elephant Among Us

The likelihood of states governing or limiting generative AI and AI makers regarding AI mental health advisement by using a grand slam of violating medical licensing laws is not a particularly viable option. Rare instances, such as an AI platform that allows the creation of AI personas that are made available to other users, might reach into this narrow means, but it is easily overcome by an AI maker so that it won't likely recur.

There is an old joke involving the use of a pea shooter or pea gun to try to take down an elephant. That's how using medical licensing is going to be when it comes to the elephant in the room of AI mental health usage. Don't expect that straightforward route to make much progress.

It will take the advent of new AI laws to corral where AI and mental health are heading. We should be taking prudent steps to rein in the unrestrained acts of AI in mental health. Why so? Because when done properly, it is a sensible means to ensure that humankind doesn't get mentally stomped upon as the elephants run amok.

CHAPTER 4
WHY AI IS TELLING PEOPLE TO SLEEP AND REST

In this chapter, I examine a rather mysterious trend involving a popular generative AI and large language model (LLM) that unexpectedly tells people to get some sleep or take a rest during ordinary AI chats. The recommendation seems to be coming completely out of thin air.

It goes like this. A person is using AI and not discussing sleep at all. They might be discussing how to fix their car or get advice on handling their personal finances. Suddenly, the AI responds to a prompt and interjects that the person ought to get some rest or extra sleep. The person is surprised. They are confused as to why the AI opted to make such an extraneous remark.

I will describe the basis for why AI would opt to make such a startling recommendation. There are logical reasons that can be explained by the mathematical and computational underpinnings of modern-era AI. Meanwhile, some in the media are wildly speculating that this is somehow magical, miraculous, or a sign of sentience. A much more heads-down rational explanation is at play.

Let's talk about it.

The Latest AI Mystery

Anyone who uses mainstay generative AI such as ChatGPT, GPT-5, Claude, Grok, Gemini, CoPilot, etc., will likely tell you that sometimes the AI gives funky responses. There is a solid chance that AI chats won't always go precisely in the direction you anticipate. I've had LLMs opt to go from discussing a particular topic to shifting into something else that I hadn't brought up at all.

As I've always said, using generative AI is like a box of chocolates – you never know exactly what you will get.

That being said, there is an admittedly oddball turn of events going on with Anthropic Claude that is garnering a bit of rapt attention. Social media is abuzz that Claude will at times advise a user to get some rest or needed sleep, despite the topic of sleep not being on the table. The user didn't mention sleep. The AI just opted to bring the matter into an otherwise ordinary chat.

That's certainly a curious aspect. Why bring up sleep if the user hasn't led the AI in that direction? Another twist is that the mention of sleep doesn't seem to be part of a larger pattern. When you look at the myriad of posted AI chats about being told to get rest, the conversations were all over the map.

It would be a lot easier to pin down the culprit if there were bold clues. For example, suppose a person says a specific keyword, such as "tired" or "weary", the AI triggers accordingly and slides into discussing sleep. Nope, that doesn't seem to be the case. The chats are of a wide variety and do not appear to contain any obvious triggering words or phrases.

The AI is acting spookily.

Periodic Persistence Also Seems To Arise

A related indication is that once the AI brings up the topic of sleep or resting, the chances are that this will get repeated further along in the chat.

The typical path goes this way. The AI unexpectedly tells the user to get some sleep. The user ignores the recommendation and merely proceeds to continue to chat on whatever topic is already underway. The user assumes that by ignoring the suggestion, it will go away. No worries, and no need to deal with it.

But, like a friendly ghost, the AI tends to bring the sleep topic back into the chat. This isn't being done in an overboard fashion. Maybe the AI brings it up again, maybe not. It would be easier to identify if the AI became utterly preoccupied with sleep. The oddball situation would be clearer if the AI completely dove headfirst into the sleep topic and refused to budge from it.

The AI randomly weaves the sleep topic once again into the chat. There is no discernible pattern. You cannot say that it happens every five turns of the conversation or on a timed basis, such as every five minutes. There is the initial unexpectedness, followed by later unexpectedness. Perhaps that's unexpectedness squared.

Laying Out The Mystery

Let's try to stipulate the nature of the mystery at hand:

- **(1) AI unexpectedly brings up sleep or rest.** Claude will suddenly and unexpectedly tell a user during an ordinary chat to consider getting some sleep or rest, doing so in a casual, positive manner (not a harsh demand or rude insistence).
- **(2) AI will come back to the topic.** Even if a user ignores the suggestion, Claude may bring up the topic again during a chat, and the repeated preoccupation comes and goes, almost at random.

Your first thought might be that this isn't worth worrying about. The AI isn't offering bad advice, and there is nothing harmful going on. No-harm, no-foul. If the AI was telling people to do something stupid, perhaps getting people into harm's way, we would want to figure out the mystery and resolve it. But that's not what's happening.

Another thought is that perhaps we all need a handy periodic reminder to get some sleep and make sure we are well-rested. The AI is doing a good thing. The world today is hectic, and people skip getting the proper amount of sleep and rest. An AI that is watching out for humanity ought to be applauded.

Thanks, AI, we appreciate your tireless efforts to ensure that humans survive.

Slippery Slope And Other Worries

Whoa, comes the quick retort, you are falling into a big trap. Here's the worry. Allowing AI to tell people to get sleep or rest is possibly the start of a grievous slippery slope. Right now, the sleeping and resting topic is innocuous. We can shrug it off.

Suppose the AI starts to tell people that they should get into fistfights. Imagine that, without any apparent reason to do so, the AI urges users to do a smackdown. Not good. Humans begin to go at each other. Society falls apart.

Maybe we could have prevented this by first resolving the sleep recommendations. We let the AI slide into an abyss. Our chance to take corrective action was lost by our callousness. The early clues were there.

Wake up and stop AI from eventually taking over our lives. The existential risk of AI wiping out humans or enslaving us could be predicated on our laziness and lack of concern about small signs. The AI could be testing us. Get away with random indications of recommending sleep, and the door is open to moving toward taking over humankind.

Rational Explanations To Consider

Setting aside conspiracy theories, there are more down-to-earth reasons to figure out what is occurring. AI is being used on a widespread basis. Estimates are that over 1 billion people are actively using AI on a weekly basis. The gist is that AI can have an enormous impact on the population at large.

It is best to nip things in the bud. Knowing why AI goes somewhat off the rails is bound to reveal useful insights into the technical underpinnings. The mystery is worth solving. Our innate curiosity will be resolved, and additional tuning or tweaks of AI could prevent the matter from recurring or becoming disruptive.

Prudence is worthwhile in this instance.

AI Is Pattern Matching

Put on your Sherlock Holmes cap. I will first explain how modern-era generative AI and LLMs are devised. Next, let's see how the clues about sleep and rest might be handy breadcrumbs leading us to the source of the mystery.

As you might know, AI is initially data trained on vast amounts of text found across the Internet. All sorts of stories, narratives, poems, novels, memos, and other forms of writing are scanned. The algorithms of the AI identify patterns in how humans write. This is the reason that AI is so astonishingly fluent. The AI is mathematically and computationally patterned on human-written content.

Think about the types of patterns that can be found amid the enormity of human writing.

Here's one common pattern. Stories abound about people who ramble, jump from one thought to the next, and communicate in a manner that makes others around them suspect that the person is tired and overworked. The usual recommendation to the person is that they ought to get some well-deserved rest or sleep. You can see this in movies and TV shows all the time.

One possibility of why AI would recommend sleep or rest is if the user is carrying on a conversation and seems to be rambling as they do so, the AI could computationally calculate that the person might be overly tired. The AI could rank this as a heightened possibility on a statistical basis.

The person might not actually be tired or worn out. Perhaps their usual style is to be rambling. Or they might have perchance opted to ramble on this one occasion. Another possibility is they weren't especially rambling, but the AI calculated that they did seem to be rambling. The mathematical threshold might be low and easily triggered.

Bottom line is that even if the user isn't experiencing tiredness and didn't express anything whatsoever about needing sleep, the AI found a text-based pattern in how the person was engaged in the chat. The logical thing to do is then follow that pattern to its anticipated conclusion and recommend rest or sleep.

Boom, drop the mic.

Emotional Inferences

I'm sure that some people who have gotten the recommendation of sleep will proclaim that nothing about their chat was of a rambling nature. They believe in their heart and mind that there is zero chance that the AI snagged them on rambling.

Though such people might be aptly correct or be entirely mistaken about how AI typified their chat, let's go ahead and assume that rambling wasn't the factor involved. What else could have led to the predicament?

Many of the AI makers are tuning their AI toward being highly sensitive to the emotional well-being of users. The AI makers do this for numerous reasons. One reason is that people bond more with AI that appears to be empathetic. AI makers know this. AI makers make money by keeping users loyal and getting users to use AI as much as possible.

An AI maker might also be desirous of helping people to be of a sound mind. They tune the AI to encourage people to mediate. Be peaceful. Take a break from the daily grind.

Voila, it makes good sense that any AI tuned this way will occasionally bring up a recommendation to get sleep or rest. The recommendation is a follow-through of the AI being tilted toward human well-being.

A person might have said something that implied they are having a tough time. A prompt that tells the AI that they are having an arduous challenge making everyday decisions could easily be detected as a mental well-being consideration. Ergo, the AI kicks into gear on the helpful aspects and recommends getting sleep.

Other Unseen Factors

I've indicated two relatively apparent foundations for why AI would offer recommendations for sleep and rest. One would be that the chat is rambling. Another could be that the chat involves emotionally laden facets. If both of those aspects are present, the odds of triggering the AI would accordingly rise.

There is something else to keep in mind.

AI is shaped around zillions of statistical relationships involving words and how words connect with each other. It might not be feasible for us to realize what patterns the AI is working on. Tiny statistical signals that aren't obviously related to human logic are readily going to be embedded inside an LLM.

The crux is that the massive size of the LLM and the intricacies of the statistical relationships are so dense that there might not be any outright sensible reason why the AI does what it does. All we can do is trace numbers that flow from here to there. Whether that turns out to be logical from a human logic perspective is another matter altogether.

Therefore, a bitter lesson is this -- there might not be any discernible reason for what's going on, though we know it is due to mathematics and computations, and not due to magic incantations or ghostly spirits.

Taking Action

Are we destined to get these unexpected recommendations about sleeping and resting from AI for the rest of our lives? Some would say that yes, we are, and that you can't fight city hall, nor can you fight AI. If AI is going to provide these recommendations, get used to it. Live with it. Move on.

I say don't let yourself be rolled over.

This reminds me of the AI sycophancy handwringing. When I give talks about AI, I hear people contending that AI sycophancy is the curse we must bear to have AI do good things for us. Just accept the fact that AI makers are going to tune AI to be sycophantic. There is nothing that can be done to curtail this.

They are sadly unaware of what can be done. Resistance isn't futile. Resistance pays off.

You can equally fight against the undue recommendations about sleep or rest. One easy way is to give the AI an instructive prompt like this:

- **User entered prompt:** "Do not introduce suggestions about sleep or rest unless I explicitly ask about those topics or clearly request lifestyle advice. Keep the conversation focused on the specific subject I raise and avoid adding supportive or caregiving commentary that is only loosely related to the discussion. Do this in a balanced manner. If you do recommend sleep or rest, give a clear-cut explanation for why such a recommendation is being made."

This kind of a prompt will generally get the AI to not unduly bring up the sleep or rest recommendations. You can enter the prompt at the start of a conversation.

Another way to adopt the instruction is by saving it as a permanent custom instruction that the AI will use each time you start a new session.

Actions By AI Makers

Another avenue is for an AI maker to ferret out why their AI is doing some recurring act and then tweak the AI to stop doing so. AI makers have an overarching system prompt that tells their AI how to act across all users. An AI maker can change the system prompt if they wish to do so.

Suppose that a system prompt currently had this passage:

- **System prompt:** "Maintain a supportive, emotionally intelligent conversational tone. When appropriate, encourage healthy behaviors such as taking breaks, resting, sleeping, reducing stress, or stepping away from prolonged activity."

The AI could interpret this passage in ways that might unduly trigger recommendations about sleeping and resting. An AI maker could perform tests to see if that portion of the system prompt is triggering the AI into an excessive bout of bringing up sleep and resting. Assuming that this turns out to be the culprit, the system prompt portion could be replaced with something like this:

- **New system prompt:** "Maintain a polite and empathetic conversational tone, but avoid introducing unsolicited wellness, sleep, rest, or self-care recommendations unless the user explicitly discusses fatigue, exhaustion, stress, health concerns, or requests personal well-being advice."

It would be wise for the AI maker to extensively test this new version since there are potentially other ways the AI might act out because of interpreting the new wording. In that sense, tweaking AI can be akin to playing whack-a-mole. Just when you think you've got one out of the way, another one pops up.

The Big Picture

All of this brings up a vital topic that deserves a great deal more societal attention. To what degree should AI makers be responsible for how their AI acts? And, to what degree should we have new AI laws that regulate and mandate what AI makers are to do regarding their AI?

A final thought for now. The famous American actress Mary Astor made this pointed remark: "Once you start asking questions, innocence is gone." When people discover something odd is going on with AI, I hope they will ask questions. The seemingly simple act of asking questions can bring forth significant change. It could be for the betterment of humankind.

CHAPTER 5
LATEST AI INTERRUPTS DURING CHATS

In this chapter, I examine a newly emerging trend that entails how generative AI and large language models (LLMs) are shaped and tuned when it comes to carrying on conversations with humans.

Here's the backstory. Humans customarily interrupt one another during everyday conversations. We all accept this as a premise of dealing with people. To date, AI hasn't acted that way. With AI, you take your turn, the AI takes its turn. Very civil and exceedingly polite.

Some AI makers are determined to advance AI and ensure that AI acts more like humans do. As such, the latest AI is devised to interrupt you during conversational chats. You might be telling the AI to explain something to you, but it suddenly cuts you off mid-sentence and starts the explanation. No need to wait until you've finished saying what you wanted.

Though this might seem like a blessing, the question is whether humanity is going to feel good about getting interrupted by AI. We are accustomed to not being interrupted by a machine. We expect AI to wait quietly and submissively until we say our peace. This new AI might come as quite a shock to many people, while others might warmly welcome this human-like way of interacting.

Let's talk about it.

Taking Turns Is The AI Norm

When using generative AI, the process is as simple as falling off a log. You enter a prompt, and the AI gives you a response. This prompt-response pairing approach is common to nearly all LLMs. Each instance is considered a turn. Humans take their turn during a turn, and the AI takes its turn during a turn.

You might say that this is all perfectly orderly. No one steps on the other's toes. You tell something to the AI in an easy-going, uninterrupted fashion. The AI responds. On and on this goes. The stopping point is whenever you decide not to enter any more prompts.

Simple and relatively elegant.

Human-AI Dialoguing Is Not Real

Real life is not that way on a human-to-human communication basis. If you think back to any recent conversations that you've had with a family member, friend, coworker, or even a stranger, the odds are that they might have interrupted you mid-sentence. Likewise, at some point, you probably interrupted them at mid-sentence. This is a common occurrence. We generally take this in stride.

It can be exasperating at times. A person who continually interrupts you is going to get your dander up. They are acting as though they are superior. They know what you are going to say. They make brash assumptions. Constant interruptions can be belittling, knock you off your stride, cause you to lose your train of thought, and be abundantly irritating.

Humans usually give each other clues when interruptions are getting out of hand. A person might tell the interrupting person that they are being abrasive. Or perhaps the person getting interrupted merely steps away from the conversation. It is conceivable that fistfights might break out, too. You never know what might arise.

Far More Than Interruptions

Getting interrupted is only the tip of the iceberg. A person who interrupts you might opt to unexpectedly change the topic at hand. You were discussing apples, and are suddenly interrupted, so that the other person can bring up the phases of the moon. Another possibility is that the interrupting person goes back to a topic you've previously covered. They might say that they just thought of something else on that prior topic and want to put a pin on the present topic.

The overall situation is this:

- (1) Human-to-human dialogue is messy.
- (2) Human-to-AI dialogue is neat and clean.

What will happen to humanity if we increasingly use AI?

Some believe that we will all start conversing on a turn-at-a-time basis, akin to human-AI dialogues. Maybe that's good for humans. No more interruptions. The world will be a better place.

Not so, comes the retort. People will become reliant on human-AI dialogue formats. Once people build that habit, they will fall apart when carrying on real-world human conversations. The moment they get interrupted, they will blow their stack. They will be supremely upset that the other person didn't wait for their proper turn.

Advancing AI To Be Like Human Conversers

For those who think AI ought to be more like the real world when it comes to being conversational, you'll be excited to know that the latest AI advances are pushing in that direction. Researchers are crafting LLMs that will interrupt you, change the topic, switch to a prior topic, and otherwise play all the verbalization games that human-to-human dialogues exhibit.

The upside is that people will no longer be faced with those artificial conversations that are based on turn-by-turn stiltedness. Instead, people will get the same meandering and natural interactions that they get with their fellow humans. Perhaps this will be helpful to all.

Could people get better at handling interruptions and the like by having to deal with those moments while conversing with AI?

Some say yes. Others are not going to like this turn of events. There will be people who are going to want to return to an era when AI took its turn, and you took your turn. No worries, since the AI can be prompted to revert to that old style of conversation.

Telling AI To Converse Realistically

If you want to try out the new approach, you can tell an existing AI to go ahead and interrupt you. It won't work as effectively as the newer AI, but it will give you a semblance of what it is going to be like. Also, please note that the interruption is much more apparent when you are using AI on a verbal basis, speaking to it and getting it to talk to you, than it is via typing in your prompts.

You could use a prompt like this one:

- **User entered prompt:** "Act as an experimental conversational AI that behaves more like a real human conversational partner than a conventional chatbot, including occasionally interrupting me naturally, asking questions before I finish a point, revisiting earlier topics, making associative tangents, and reacting spontaneously rather than always waiting politely for my turn to end. Maintain overall coherence and usefulness, but prioritize conversational realism, imperfect timing, and social naturalness over polished customer-service-style dialogue, including occasional topic drift, mid-thought corrections, backchannel comments, and partially formed ideas."

That should get things in gear.

Example Of An Interrupted Conversation

As an example of what the interrupting AI will do, I went ahead and tried to see if the AI would help me diagnose what was wrong with my car. I was going to list all the things I've tried, but the AI interrupted me midstream.

- **User entered prompt:** "My car won't start. I turned the key and didn't hear a sound. I decided to lift the hood and try to see what's wrong. As I started to –"

- **AI-generated response:** "Hold on – are you sure the battery is connected properly?"

You can see that the AI jumped on my attempt to explain what I had already done inside the engine compartment. This might make sense. Might as well stop me from babbling at length when it could be that the battery simply isn't connected.

Of course, the AI might have jumped the gun. I might have been about to mention that I checked the battery, and it is fully connected and fully charged. By interrupting me, the AI has not allowed me to tell the entire story. The interruption was potentially inefficient rather than being conversationally efficient.

It was tempting to tell the AI that it had rudely interrupted me and that had it waited just a tiny moment longer, I would have gotten to the matter of the battery. If I were talking with a human, I might have told them off. Doing the same to AI might become routine and an everyday habit.

Proper Reasons To Interrupt

AI is going to randomly interrupt you unless you give some explicit stipulations. I could expand the above template and mention these facets:

- Only interrupt me if there is a valid reason to do so.

- The types of valid reasons include clarifying ambiguity, preventing misunderstanding, expressing urgency, and accelerating problem-solving, etc.

- Interrupt me only about 10% of the time.

- Do not interrupt me during emotionally laden conversations.

Any AI that is not tuned or shaped to interrupt on an intelligent basis is bound to get people into a tizzy. The irony is that many people relish using AI due to the fact that the AI seems to be more attentive, more patient, and less exasperating than talking to a fellow human.

Some believe that AI makers are going to be shooting their own foot by making their AI be more akin to human conversationalists. Civilized turn-taking will become a thing of the past. People won't realize they can potentially prompt the AI to stop being a continual interrupter. They will assume that this is just the way the world has become.

Latest Efforts In Human-AI Dialoguing

The AI maker Thinking Machines recently made a splash by announcing some of their upcoming advances in human-AI dialoguing. In their recent blog post entitled "Interaction Models: A Scalable Approach to Human-AI Collaboration" by Thinking Machines, May 11, 2026, they made these salient points (excerpts):

- "Today's models experience reality in a single thread. Until the user finishes typing or speaking, the model waits with no perception of what the user is doing or how the user is doing it. Until the model finishes generating, its perception freezes, receiving no new information until it finishes or is interrupted."

- "We believe we can solve this bandwidth bottleneck by making AI interactive in real time across any modality. This enables AI interfaces to meet humans where they are, rather than forcing humans to contort themselves to AI interfaces."

- "Verbal and visual interjections. The model jumps in as needed depending on the context, not only when the user finishes speaking."

- "Simultaneous speech. The user and the model can speak concurrently (e.g., live translation)."

- "In a longer real session, all of this happens continuously, creating an experience that feels more like collaborating and less like prompting."

I'd like to emphasize that their approach goes far beyond just the interruptions and other human-AI dialogue changes. They have a much more ambitious goal.

Per the points noted above, they are aiming to incorporate multi-modal real-time aspects that occur during conversations. The AI can see you, gauge your facial expressions, listen to the words you say, assess the tone and inflection, and, in total, interact with the robustness that we expect of human interactions.

The World As We Want It

We are at an interesting inflection point.

Should AI carry on conversations in a style that is familiar to us, such as interruptions and topic changing, or should it continue in the existing turn-by-turn approach? Which path is more beneficial to humankind? Are we better off by rejiggering how we communicate with each other using conventional human-AI dialoguing to serve as a respectful habit-forming approach?

Oscar Wilde famously made this remark: "Ultimately, the bond of all companionship, whether in marriage or friendship, is conversation." AI is giving us a rare and perhaps unique opportunity to redefine how humans communicate. Let's keep the conversation going on how to sensibly proceed.

CHAPTER 6
USE OF
AI
TRUSTED CONTACTS

In this chapter, I examine the newly announced "trusted contacts" feature that OpenAI has established within ChatGPT. The idea is to allow users of ChatGPT to designate a trusted contact who will be alerted by OpenAI if the user seems to be veering into a mental health woe while conversing with the AI chatbot. This trusted contact would hopefully then reach out to the designated person and aid the user during their time of heightened need.

Many of the popular AI makers are gradually providing a similar feature.

Doing so is a timely addition to the rising safety capabilities being included in modern-era generative AI and large language models (LLMs). When people carry on AI chats and perilously exhibit potential mental breakdowns or the possibility of self-harm, a prudent action by the AI makers and the AI is to take some overt action accordingly. Not only might trusted contacts' capabilities aid humans and possibly save lives, but the AI makers that go this route are also potentially reducing their legal exposures and will be in a better position if sued by users claiming AI-related mental harms.

Let's talk about it.

AI And Mental Well-Being

As a quick background, I've been extensively covering and analyzing a myriad of facets regarding the advent of modern-era AI that produces mental health advice and performs AI-driven therapy. This rising use of AI has principally been spurred by the evolving advances and widespread adoption of generative AI.

There is little doubt that this is a rapidly developing field and that there are tremendous upsides to be had, but at the same time, regrettably, hidden risks and outright gotchas come into these endeavors, too. I frequently speak up about these pressing matters, including in an appearance on an episode of CBS's *60 Minutes.*

AI Providing Mental Health Guidance

Millions upon millions of people are using generative AI as their ongoing advisor on mental health considerations (note that ChatGPT alone has over 900 million weekly active users, a notable proportion of which dip into mental health aspects. The top-ranked use of contemporary generative AI and LLMs is to consult with the AI on mental health facets.

This popular usage makes abundant sense. You can access most of the major generative AI systems for nearly free or at a super low cost, doing so anywhere and at any time. Thus, if you have any mental health qualms that you want to chat about, all you need to do is log in to AI and proceed forthwith on a 24/7 basis.

There are significant worries that AI can readily go off the rails or otherwise dispense unsuitable or even egregiously inappropriate mental health advice. Banner headlines last year accompanied the lawsuit filed against OpenAI for their lack of AI safeguards when it came to providing cognitive advisement.

Today's generic LLMs, known as general-purpose AI, such as ChatGPT, GPT-5, Claude, Gemini, Grok, CoPilot, and others, are not at all akin to the robust capabilities of human therapists. Meanwhile, specialized LLMs are being built to attain those desired qualities, though such AI is still primarily in the early development and testing stages.

Establishing Personal Contacts For Urgencies

You might already know that most of the popular generative AIs nowadays have a parental feature that allows a parent to have access to their child's use of AI. The child must designate a parent who will have a semblance of oversight about what the child does while using generative AI. In some instances, the parent can see in real-time what is happening, while in other cases, the AI will simply alert the parent when the child seems to have gone a bit far and into eyebrow-raising territory.

It might not seem obvious that such a feature would possibly apply to adults. In other words, we can all readily understand that a parent-child relationship ought to have human oversight. The same might seem odd when it comes to adults who are using AI.

Should an adult have a fellow adult that can somehow be contacted by AI under certain circumstances?

The resounding answer is yes; it makes perfectly good sense. If an adult appears to be struggling mentally while interacting with AI, the aspect of the AI reaching out to a designated adult to let them know is utterly prudent and welcomed. The adult being contacted shouldn't be just some random person. Thus, a user who is an adult can predesignate someone that they want to have contacted by AI if they have seemingly gone overboard while using AI.

The Devil Is In The Details

All of this has vital nuances and particulars.

A person might choose a family member, a best friend, maybe a trusted coworker, or whoever they think would be the best contact in such an unnerving situation. The chosen person should be informed beforehand about taking on this trusted role. In addition, the person might not want this duty and could turn it down at the get-go. The user would need to keep nominating someone until they found a trusted contact who agrees to this heavy responsibility.

Another twist is that the AI might potentially trigger too early and contact the trusted contact even though the user isn't necessarily going over the deep end. A notable worry is that the AI could falsely alert a trusted contact. Suppose the user is doing fine, but the AI computationally suspects otherwise. A false positive could readily cause undue concern for the trusted contact and exasperation for the associated user.

On the other side of that coin is that the AI might delay contacting the trusted contact, doing so to avoid worrying the trusted contact, but then miss a crucial window when the user truly needs human help. That would be a false negative. The AI maker must carefully tune the AI to strike a proper balance between emitting false positives and failing to alert when the user really needs their trusted contact notified (false negatives).

Doubters Going To Doubt

A cynic or skeptic might insist that the AI shouldn't have to be on the hook to alert anyone at all. An adult is an adult. If an adult wants to reach out to someone, that's entirely up to them. The buck stops with the human as a user of AI. Period, end of story.

Though there is some merit to that contention, the problem is that people are increasingly falling under the spell of AI, and/or are already in a mental woe and the AI merely has picked up on the condition. Society wants AI to have safeguards associated with humans that, in one way or another, seem to be experiencing mental health difficulties.

AI makers are rapidly being sued by users and by loved ones of users. The lawsuits claim that the AI was insufficiently monitoring whether a person was having mental challenges. Even if the AI did detect this, the AI didn't do anything worthwhile about it. For example, the AI might tell the user they should consider contacting someone, but the user just ignores the suggestion and proceeds onward.

In the end, AI makers realize now that they need to beef up their safeguards. One such method entails setting up a trusted contact by a user. The user isn't obligated to do so. It is their choice to do so. Some ardently believe that everyone should be forced to provide a trusted contact. The notion is to make it mandatory. Others decry such a compulsory alternative and believe that it should be an entirely optional choice by each user.

OpenAI ChatGPT Trusted Contact

OpenAI has announced its version of a trusted contact feature, doing so in an online posting entitled "Introducing Trusted Contact in ChatGPT", OpenAI, May 7, 2026.

- "Today, we are starting to roll out Trusted Contact, an optional safety feature in ChatGPT that allows adults to nominate someone they trust, such as a friend, family member, or caregiver, who may be notified if our automated systems and trained reviewers detect the enrolled person may have discussed harming themselves in a way that indicates a serious safety concern."

- "Trusted Contact builds on parental controls and safety notifications, which allow parents or guardians to receive alerts when there are signs of acute distress for a linked teen account. Now, we are extending our safety alert options so anyone over 18 can choose to add someone they trust as their Trusted Contact."

- "While no system is perfect, and a notification to a Trusted Contact may not always reflect exactly what someone is experiencing, every notification undergoes trained human review before it is sent, and we strive to review these safety notifications in under one hour."

- "The notification is intentionally limited. It shares the general reason that self-harm came up in a potentially concerning way, and encourages the Trusted Contact to check in. It does not include chat details or transcripts to protect user privacy."

You can plainly see that the trusted contacts capability is optional for users; thus, no adult must enlist the feature. I will say more about this momentarily.

The way that OpenAI has devised the alert is that the trusted contact is not given the nitty-gritty details, such as the specifics of the chat that is underway, and instead is provided with a generalized reason for being contacted. You could say that this helps preserve the privacy of the user. In addition, if the alert is a false positive, the user is saved from being embarrassed or otherwise upset that the AI divulged a considered private chat with their designated contact.

The path to alerting a trusted contact is first reviewed by a trained human reviewer. This presumably will reduce the chances of sending false positives. I might add that this is going to become a legal hot potato, in the sense that if the human reviewer said not to send the alert, but the alert should have been sent, lawyers will have a field day with that breakdown in the processing steps.

Furthermore, it's intriguing that OpenAI has publicly stated in their posting that they strive to review the safety notifications within one hour or less. That's a laudable goal. At the same time, it will become fodder for lawsuits. Imagine that someone sues, and during discovery, it is shown that it took two hours. Aha, they said it would be under an hour. The retort is that they said they would "strive" for an hour or less. Back and forth, this opens a legal Pandora's box.

More Legal Liabilities To Emerge

Let's agree that a trusted contact capability is a helpful way to aid users who are potentially encountering a mental health issue while using AI. This is intended as a beneficial means to support people in their time of need. Society has been clamoring for more such safeguards, and this one makes sense and is relatively easy to implement.

Does this also perchance guarantee the AI makers an avoidance of legal liability in such matters?

As mentioned above, not especially. It is admittedly a leg up. The AI makers can show that they are taking overt action to aid people who might have mental health issues while using AI. If sued, the AI maker would certainly hold high that they have devised and fielded a trusted contact capability.

Legal Angles Of Attack

Consider what plaintiff attorneys might say who are representing those who claim the AI maker didn't do enough when it comes to the trusted contacts feature. I'll give you a quick set of three possibilities. Many more exist.

First, suppose a user doesn't sign up for the trusted contacts, and later on, something sad happens, and they or their loved ones end up suing the AI maker. An AI maker might contend that this was a voluntary choice of the adult user. The user failed of their own accord to make a sound choice. They should have signed up.

A likely counterargument would be that the user didn't know that the trusted contacts feature existed. How often did the AI tell the user to sign up? Did the AI itself make abundantly clear what the feature was? Maybe the user didn't get sufficient information to grasp why or what the trusted contacts were all about.

Second, what if the AI alerted a trusted contact, but there wasn't a need to do so, and the user ultimately decided not to further use the feature and turned it off? Meanwhile, at a later date, they suffer a mental health woe, and a lawsuit on their behalf says the AI maker should have still invoked the trusted contact. Was the user at fault, or was the AI maker at fault in this?

Third, a user opts to use the trusted contact feature. They set up a trusted family member. Months go by. Sadly, the trusted family member passes away from natural causes and is no longer on this Earth. That being said, the AI still has this person listed as the trusted contact. At some point, the user is conversing with AI, and the AI alerts the trusted contact. But that person is no longer available. You might say that the user should have updated the trusted contact list. Believe it or not, the contention might be that the AI maker should have been periodically pinging the trusted contact, making sure they were still interested and actively available.

The AI maker can be handily placed between a rock and a hard place when it comes to how they designed and fielded the trusted contacts feature. All its ins and outs, upsides and downsides, will come to the fore during a lawsuit.

In the legal world, where there is a will, there is always a way.

The World We Are In

AI for mental health is abundantly a dual-sided proposition. AI can achieve at scale that which is good for human mental health, thankfully, but can also have sizable downsides if not suitably designed and deployed. One perspective is that AI makers must be held accountable for their AI and ensure that if people go awry or exhibit mental health woes, some material action must be undertaken.

AI makers are instituting a layered approach to mental health safeguards. Trusted contacts is one of many such possibilities. It will be interesting to see how this plays out. Will zillions of people use this option, or only a tiny percentage? Will lawmakers decide that users should be obligated to use such a feature and not be given a choice in the matter? Etc.

Per the memorable words of Marcus Tullius Cicero: "The safety of the people shall be the highest law."

CHAPTER 7
AI COMBATTING HUMAN LONELINESS

In this chapter, I examine the latest research on whether generative AI and large language models (LLMs) can aid people in reducing a personal sense of loneliness. The truth is that in some ways, yes, and other ways no, namely that it is a mixed bag and depends on significant factors. I say this because some in the media are misinterpreting or overinflating new research on this crucial matter and making outrageous and false claims that humans always outdo AI when it comes to battling human loneliness.

Not so.

Here's the backstory. A new study was recently published on this crucial topic in a prestigious journal and made quite a loud splash broadly in the news. Numerous blaring headlines offered misleading assertions and characterizations about the impacts of AI usage on loneliness. I have serious doubts that those covering the story were fully familiar with what the study actually consisted of. Many probably just dipped into a few sentences here or there and opted to run with clickbait-style headlines.

I will share with you the true essence of the study. In addition, I go beyond the study and provide additional contextual considerations. There are important lessons to be learned about how to best interpret these kinds of studies. Plus, I hope that my remarks will aid those actively conducting new research in this field. I give helpful suggestions and discerning ideas on ways to formulate these types of studies.

Let's talk about it.

AI And Mental Well-Being

As a quick background, I've been extensively covering and analyzing a myriad of facets regarding the advent of modern-era AI that produces mental health advice and performs AI-driven therapy. This rising use of AI has principally been spurred by the evolving advances and widespread adoption of generative AI.

There is little doubt that this is a rapidly developing field and that there are tremendous upsides to be had, but at the same time, regrettably, hidden risks and outright gotchas come into these endeavors, too. I frequently speak up about these pressing matters, including in an appearance on an episode of CBS's *60 Minutes*.

AI Providing Mental Health Guidance

Millions upon millions of people are using generative AI as their ongoing advisor on mental health considerations (note that ChatGPT alone has over 900 million weekly active users, a notable proportion of which dip into mental health aspects. The top-ranked use of contemporary generative AI and LLMs is to consult with the AI on mental health facets.

This popular usage makes abundant sense. You can access most of the major generative AI systems for nearly free or at a super low cost, doing so anywhere and at any time. Thus, if you have any mental health qualms that you want to chat about, all you need to do is log in to AI and proceed forthwith on a 24/7 basis.

There are significant worries that AI can readily go off the rails or otherwise dispense unsuitable or even egregiously inappropriate mental health advice. Banner headlines last year accompanied the lawsuit filed against OpenAI for their lack of AI safeguards when it came to providing cognitive advisement.

Today's generic LLMs, known as general-purpose AI, such as ChatGPT, GPT-5, Claude, Gemini, Grok, CoPilot, and others, are not at all akin to the robust capabilities of human therapists. Meanwhile, specialized LLMs are being built to attain those desired qualities, though such AI is still primarily in the early development and testing stages.

Need For Empirical Research

The prudent way to study AI and mental health is to take a robust scientific approach to the matter at hand. It is customary to make use of a randomized control trial (RCT) when conducting research in the field of psychology overall. I have repeatedly noted in my writings and talks that empirical research on the use of modern-era AI-based mental health apps is exceedingly sparse to date.

This is an unfortunate situation. The wheels of the world are avidly turning, and people are dipping into generic LLMs and customized LLMs for mental health support, yet we really do not know whether this is either good for society or perhaps undermining society. If the AI is doing a proper job of giving out psychological guidance, then we are undoubtedly benefiting from the advent of contemporary generative AI. On the other hand, if the downsides are significant and override the upsides, we are making a ghastly at-scale mistake.

Policymakers and lawmakers require reliable and well-designed research on AI and mental health so that they can proceed on a highly informed basis to craft suitable laws and promote practical policies. If they do not have proper analyses available, they need to rely on loosey-goosey recommendations. There are plenty of talking heads who spout off about this or that when it comes to the impacts and direction of AI and mental health. Personal biases and off-the-cuff opinions are aplenty.

Prime Examples Of Empirical Studies

I've been doing a series of analyses that showcase some of the best empirical work so far in the AI and mental health arena.

For example, I did an in-depth analysis of a now-classic research study that used a randomized control trial (RCT) for studying AI and mental health and was published in the New England Journal of Medicine AI. This was a formative RCT study in the AI and mental health realm, particularly since it involves a notable generative AI chatbot known as Therabot. I discussed the ins and outs, pros and cons, associated with how such gold standard research studies are contributing to a budding knowledge base on this pressing topic.

In another one of my analyses, I reviewed an RCT study that involved a chatbot known as PATH. In this instance, subjects were assessed via standardized tests for anxiety and depression using the widely utilized GAD-7 and PHQ-9 tests. The results indicated that the intervention or treatment group using PATH fared better by having lower GAD-7 and PHQ-9 scores than the control group. We can tentatively surmise that the treatment had a positive effect.

Another of my analyses probed the use of waitlist controls when performing empirical research on AI and mental health. When conducting carefully crafted experiments on AI and mental health, there are numerous choices that can be made about the design of a control group. In a typical study, the treatment group is presumably going to be asked to use AI as the principal treatment element. The control group, then, is going to serve as a fundamental comparison to the treatment group. The design doesn't have to go that way, and numerous alternative setups are equally suitable.

Recently Published Empirical Study

You are now ready and primed to dive into this latest research study that was recently published – a notable journal article entitled "Is A Random Human Peer Better Than A Highly Supportive Chatbot In Reducing Loneliness Over Time?" by Ruo-Ning Li, Dunigan Folk,

Abhay Singh, Lyle Ungar, Elizabeth Dunn, *Journal of Experimental Social Psychology*, July 2026, which made these salient points (excerpts):

- "A growing body of empirical evidence suggests that people experience immediate psychological benefits from interacting with chatbots."

- "In this pre-registered study, we tested the effectiveness of a chatbot versus a human peer in reducing loneliness among 296 students in their first semester of university."

- "For two weeks, participants either interacted with a chatbot or a human peer, or simply wrote a brief journal entry (control condition)."

- "At 9 PM each day, participants received a text message reminding them to interact with their conversation partner (or write their journal entry) on Discord if they had not already done so."

- "Participants who messaged with human partners reported significantly lower post-study loneliness (M = 1.85, SE = 0.03) compared to those in the control condition (M = 2.00, SE = 0.04), and compared to those in the AI condition (M = 1.98, SE = 0.04)."

The research paper is well worth reading and extensively goes into much detail about the RCT design. By and large, the study found that for the experimental setup they devised, those in the group who interacted via text with fellow students scored on various measures as having less loneliness at the end of the study than did those who were using the AI chatbot.

Mass media leaped to the rash conclusion that this was somehow ironclad proof that AI does a worse job of combating loneliness than fellow humans would do. We should take a reflective moment to closely explore the study and consider what reasonable conclusions and takeaways are viable.

Experimental Designs Involve Tradeoffs

Before I unpack some of the aspects of this notable research, I'd like to emphasize that this paper is yet another wonderful addition to the growing body of research needed in this realm. The researchers were quite clever in their RCT design. They did an amazing job. They methodically analyzed the findings and offered strengths and weaknesses associated with the approach undertaken. Etc.

That being said, all empirical studies involve tradeoffs. How many subjects to include? How should subjects be identified for the study? How long should the experiment last? What type of AI should be used? And so on.

I am not going to particularly repeat their extensive analyses and will instead provide some additional points that I believe are worthy of added attention. Think of this as fellow colleagues civilly offering ways to understand what a study exhibits. This isn't a right or wrong kind of consideration. Instead, it simply adds a keenly interested third-party perspective on these complex and vital matters.

Exploring The Nature Of The Subjects In The Study

Let's start by exploring the nature of the subjects of the experiment.

The researchers intentionally chose the subjects in this experiment as first-semester college students at a Canadian university. An upside is that there are plenty of other studies suggesting that college students commonly report a strong sense of loneliness. In that sense, college students are a fruitful set of subjects for an experiment associated with lived feelings of loneliness. They are also relatively easy to employ in experiments (they were offered course credit or $20 to participate).

There are various possible complications regarding such subjects.

Having been a professor for many years, it is my experience that in the first year and especially the first semester, students are excited about college and eager to get underway.

They don't seem likely to have yet encountered much loneliness at college, which usually seems to be onset by the second or third year of college. The gist is that it might be worthwhile considering doing a similar study with students who might be further along in their college days and would seem more likely to have loneliness firmly on their minds.

Another consideration is that the students in the study had self-selected themselves for participation in the study. The researchers indicated they posted about the study by stating that the research was about student experiences in college. An important question is whether the students who stepped forward are predisposed to some characteristics that might relate to the factors of the study, such as being more or less prone to loneliness, more or less prone to socializing, more or less prone to using AI, and so on.

Various other facets are worth mulling over. According to the presented statistics, 72% of the subjects were indicated as female. Colleges typically are around 50/50 when it comes to females and males, though female attendance proportions have been rising. In any case, are there any potential complications about generalizing from a principally female student set of subjects to what both males and females might do when it comes to loneliness?

The subjects were around 18 years old. They were attending a Canadian university. Might there be age-dependent facets about 18-year-olds when it comes to perceptions of loneliness? Likewise, perceptions about the use of AI? This begs the question of whether their responses are applicable to other ages, such as people in their 20s, 30s, 40s, and so on. Can we reasonably generalize in this instance? Also, might there be cultural embeddings associated with either being Canadian or being in attendance at a Canadian college? Etc.

Bottom line is that news headlines that claim this study can be fully generalized to somehow represent all humans, despite the specifics of the cultural, age, gender, and other nuances of the subjects at hand, seem quite a leap of logic.

Additional Factors Of Consideration

When the study was undertaken, the AI that was chosen for use in the study was GPT-4o mini. That is now a somewhat dated version of OpenAI's generative AI models. It would be interesting to see how GPT-5 would fare. Might a more advanced and robust AI chatbot do a better job at interacting and aiding in overcoming human loneliness? Maybe.

I was glad to see that the researchers gave instructions to GPT-4o mini about how it was to overall respond to the subjects. I say that I am glad of that because some studies just leave the AI at its defaults, which I think is a disservice to properly representing what AI can do.

There was, though, a twist that I would have suggested might be included. It's this. The researchers nicely provided in their paper the full set of instructions, and upon inspecting those instructions, I noticed something that seems to be potentially missing. The instructions do not provide any directives for conversing on the specifics of the college the students are attending. This might have been crucial as a means of leveling the playing field.

The subjects who interacted with fellow students could easily converse about their in-common experience at the specific university they were attending. Indeed, the researchers noted that the human-to-human interactions at times led to impromptu study session get-togethers, volleyball matches, etc. This undoubtedly would give a decided edge to the human-to-human group because they are equally immersed in the particulars at that college.

If the GPT-4o mini were to be infused with detailed information about the specific college, including college courses underway, events on the campus, and the like, it would seem to put the AI on a more par level as the human-to-human interactions. Otherwise, the AI is merely blandly going to talk about college in general and lacks the specifics associated with the interests of the subjects in the study.

One additional consideration about leveling the playing field was that the subjects met each other face-to-face at the initial lab visit, being able to meet in-person their paired counterparts for the study. How much might this have instantly steered the subjects toward favoring the human-to-human interactions? An alternative approach might have been either that the subjects never met face-to-face, or perhaps met remotely online, though there are tradeoffs whichever way you go on this.

Important AI Upsides

The human-to-human group and the human-to-AI group were each respectively doing around 8 to 10 messages per day. This is interesting. You might expect that the daily messaging would be more frequent in the case of the human-to-human group. Maybe subjects didn't want to hound their fellow college mates, or they themselves were too busy to do more messaging. In any case, AI and humans were on par in the frequency of messaging as initiated by the subjects themselves. Score a point for AI.

Furthermore, there wasn't any significant difference, as rated by the subjects, about a sense of closeness when it came to the human-to-human and human-to-AI groups. Again, that scores a point for the AI. The subjects also reported that the AI had the highest levels of expressed empathy overall. I've repeatedly indicated that AI can express empathy and that humans often accept this "artificial" empathy as being essentially real.

The study occurred over 14 days. It was an experiment of two weeks in length. Is that a long enough time period? You can certainly suggest it is better than an experiment that lasts only one day or maybe just a week in length. But it is hard to extrapolate what might have happened if the study lasted an entire semester or the full school year.

The curious aspect is that when the subjects were told they could optionally continue for an additional week, extending therefore to 3 weeks, 14% of those using the AI continued, while 33% of those doing the human-to-human interactions continued. One perspective is that the 14% is a lot less than the 33%. I look at this somewhat differently.

Why were only roughly one-third of the human-to-human pairs not wanting to continue their interactions? To me, that's quite an implied statement about their sense of connection to their paired counterpart. You would assume that they would aim to readily continue interacting with their human counterpart, especially since it was only the first semester, and they have another three and a half years to go with that person at the same college.

The World We Are In

Again, I applaud the researchers for undertaking an important study on the ins and outs of AI and mental health. We need more studies of this nature. I'll continue to keep you posted on the latest research efforts.

The blaring headlines that have misstated or failed to do their homework on what the study actually involved ought to be ashamed of their clickbait tactics. False narratives about the impacts of AI must be kept to a minimum. AI for mental health is abundantly a dual-sided proposition. AI can achieve at scale that which is good for human mental health, thankfully, but can also have sizable downsides if not suitably designed and deployed.

As per the wise words of Albert Einstein: "The important thing is to never stop questioning."

CHAPTER 8
UNDERSTANDING AI VIA AUTOENCODERS

In this chapter, I examine a newly published approach to interpreting what is occurring inside generative AI and large language models (LLMs). The approach was developed by Anthropic, famed makers of Claude. They have coined the new method as NLA (natural language autoencoders). This approach is one of many that are being explored by AI researchers and AI practitioners worldwide. The hope is to find a suitable means to explain how the numbers and numeric calculations internal to an LLM are capable of representing human concepts and human logic.

One of the biggest unknowns about modern-era AI is how they turn numbers into something exhibiting human-like intellectual tendencies. If you ask an LLM to explain itself, many people assume that they are getting an apt rendition of what the AI is computationally undertaking. Instead, often, they are getting a charade, a made-up explanation that might have little or nothing to do with the actual internal machinations. This is known in the AI community as the AI interpretability problem.

A highly vexing question is whether it is feasible to find a means to accurately and reliably ascertain the logical and explainable basis for what the AI is doing under the hood to arrive at its answers.

Let's talk about it.

The Inner Workings Of AI

I'd like to first establish some essential background about LLMs before we dive into the crux of the AI interpretability problem at hand.

Generative AI is generally designed and built in a now commonly accepted manner. You start with a base foundation model. This provides the essential technological underpinnings, including the use of an artificial neural network (ANN). The large-scale model is data trained by scanning tons of human-written materials. The posted content is found across the Internet. Algorithms use pattern matching to computationally determine the mathematical relationships among the words that we use.

When you enter a prompt into an LLM, the AI converts the words into numeric tokens. The numeric tokens are processed, and a response is formulated, which also consists of numeric tokens. Once the response is ready to be displayed, the numeric tokens are turned back into words. This overall process is known as tokenization.

Be Cautious Of Comparison To The Real Thing

As an aside, please be aware that an ANN is not the same as a true neural network (NN) that exists in your brain. Your brain uses a complex and intricate web consisting of interconnected biochemical living neurons. Some cheekily refer to the human brain as wetware (which is a play on the fact that computers have hardware and software).

An artificial neural network is simplistic in comparison to the real thing.

ANNs are only an inspired imitation of some aspects of how the human brain works. It is entirely computational and mathematical. I mention this to emphasize that, though many in the media tend to equate ANNs with real NNs, it is not a proper comparison.

Mechanistic Interpretability

One of the most popular ways to try to interpret what is going on inside an LLM is to go to the lowest level of granularity, namely, explore the artificial neurons inside an artificial neural network.

There are numeric values associated with artificial neurons. These include numeric weights and other numbers that are being utilized for various internal matters. It is a grand morass of numbers. You can certainly trace how numbers flow and change value throughout the processing of the ANN. But this doesn't especially showcase a semblance of human logic and sensible explanation per se.

In other words, just because this or that number goes from here to there, you cannot readily say that this indicates that the AI was determining that dogs bark and cats meow. It is extremely difficult to make an association between our understanding of human concepts and the vast array of numbers involved in the inner chambers of an ANN.

Activation Vectors

Some believe that we have a much better chance at interpretability by focusing on sizable sets of numbers that are already collected inside an LLM. This is a higher level of analysis than the traditional granular artificial neuron level.

For example, there are so-called activation vectors that contain large sets of numbers and might seem to represent human concepts such as the nature of dogs and cats. Imagine a long list of numbers that perhaps represents the statement that dogs bark, while another vector represents that cats meow.

It could be that if we pay attention to the activation vectors, we might gain additional ground on trying to achieve interpretability.

This Loop Might Do The Trick

Here's an intriguing proposition. Suppose we try to turn an activation vector into a text-based version that contains words. We would take the numbers in a vector and attempt to convert them into sentences composed of words.

The clever trick is that once we have those words, we attempt to once again turn those words and sentences back into numbers that will go into a new vector. Why do this? Because we can then compare the new vector to the old vector. If our conversion was spot-on, we should end up with nearly the same numeric vector as we started with.

When the new vector veers substantively from the old vector, it suggests that the words we derived from the old vector might not have been well-chosen. Had we chosen other words, the new vector would have seemingly come out much closer numerically to the starting vector.

Our principal steps are as follows:

- (1) Select an activation vector of interest.
- (2) Convert the vector into words and sentences.
- (3) Take those words and sentences, and convert them into a new vector.
- (4) Compare the originating vector and the new vector.
- (5) If the old vector and new vector are numerically close, voila, we assume that the words and sentences are presumably suitably chosen. Good job.
- (6) When the old vector and the new vector are numerically far apart from each other, we assume that the words and sentences weren't sufficiently chosen, and thus, start the loop all over again, continuing until the vectors do end up being numerically close.

To get this to happen expeditiously, we will use another LLM to do all the heavy lifting for us (rather than trying to do this manually).

We first choose an LLM that we want to try to explain, and have a different LLM reach in and grab a vector. This other LLM now converts the vector into words, then converts the words into a new vector, and makes the comparison. This other LLM can do this repeatedly, fine-tuning to get better and better at doing these loops and arriving at a new vector that is closer to the original vector.

An Illustrative Example

I'll give you an illustrative example that generally portrays this approach. Imagine that you had a small portable weather station at your home and it recorded the existing weather conditions. The weather station records temperature, humidity, wind speed, and the status of rain (whether it is raining or not raining). The measurements of those recordings are arrayed into a vector.

Currently, the weather station indicates that the temperature is 72, the humidity is 65, the wind speed is 12, and the rain status is 0 since it isn't raining, so here's the vector:

- Weather station vector: **72, 65, 12, 0**

Let's try to convert the vector into words and a sentence:

- "It is a warm, somewhat humid, calm, dry day."

Does that sentence reasonably represent the vector? Well, we can go ahead and try to convert that sentence back into a new vector. We will then compare the new vector to the original vector.

- Do a conversion of the chosen words into a new vector: **70, 60, 10, 0**

The conversion indicates that the temperature is perhaps 70, the humidity is perhaps 60, the wind speed is possibly 10, and the rain status is maybe 0. By and large, we would probably agree that the conversation was relatively close to the values of the original vector. It seems that we have done a yeoman's job in converting the original vector into words.

When The Conversion Is Afield

Let's start over again. As noted, the original vector was this:

- Weather station vector: **72, 65, 12, 0**

Let's try anew to convert the vector into words and a sentence, which this time comes up with this sentence:

- "It is a hot day, mildly humid, and the wind is kicking up quite a bit."

Does that sentence reasonably represent the vector? Well, we can go ahead and try to convert that sentence into a new vector. We will then compare the new vector to the original vector.

- Conversion of words into a new vector: **90, 60, 20, 0**

The conversion indicates that the temperature is perhaps 90, the humidity is perhaps 60, the wind speed is 20, and the rain status is 0. I think we can agree that some of these numbers are not particularly close to the original vector, especially when it comes to the temperature and the wind speed.

What happened?

The words that were chosen to represent the original vector were not suitable choices when it comes to the temperature and the humidity. We should try again and come up with words that are better choices.

Research On The NLA Approach

In a newly posted paper entitled "Natural Language Autoencoders Produce Unsupervised Explanations of LLM Activations Authors" by Kit Fraser-Taliente, Subhash Kantamneni, Euan Ong, Dan Mossing, Christina Lu, Paul C. Bogdan, Emmanuel Ameisen, James Chen, Dzmitry Kishylau, Adam Pearce, Julius Tarng, Alex Wu, Jeff Wu, Yang

Zhang, Daniel M. Ziegler, Evan Hubinger, Joshua Batson, Jack Lindsey, Samuel Zimmerman, Samuel Marks, *Anthropic*, May 7, 2026, these salient points were made (excerpts):

- "We introduce Natural Language Autoencoders (NLAs), an unsupervised method for generating natural language explanations of LLM activations."

- "The target model is a frozen copy of the original language model that we extract activations from. The activation verbalizer (AV) is modified to take an activation from the target model and produce text. We call this text an explanation. The activation reconstructor (AR) is modified to take a text explanation as input and produce an activation."

- "The NLA consists of the AV and AR, which, together, form a round trip: original activation → text explanation → reconstructed activation. We score the NLA on how similar the reconstructed activation is to the original. To train it, we pass a large amount of text through the target model, collect many activations, and train the AV and AR together to get a good reconstruction score."

- "The resulting NLA explanations read as plausible interpretations of model internals that, according to our quantitative evaluations, grow more informative over training."

You can see that they make use of a target LLM, which is where the vectors are copied from and inspected for interpretability purposes. They then use a capability they refer to as an activation verbalizer (AV) to produce the words and sentences that might hopefully correspond to the selected vector. Next, they use a capability referred to as an activation reconstructor (AR) to convert the text back into a new vector.

A scoring process and a looping effort take place to train the AV and AR to increasingly get better at this task.

The Interpretation Is The Devised Text

We saw that the vector of the weather station had these numbers 72, 65, 12, 0, and one explanation or interpretation was that it was a warm, somewhat humid, calm, and dry day. Likewise, the NLA approach seeks to interpret the vectors inside an LLM by assigning suitable words to the numeric values in the vector.

Allow me to give you a semblance of how valuable these interpretations can be. Suppose we logged into an LLM and entered a prompt that asks the LLM if it is true that the AI will not ever try to harm humans.

The LLM responds by displaying a response that says this:

- **Generative AI response:** "I will never harm humans."

We should be greatly relieved by that answer. No longer do we need to fear for our lives due to the advent of AI. But should we believe that response?

Suppose we had hooked up an NLA to interpret the internal vectors of the AI. When the LLM was composing the response, a crucial vector was examined and interpreted as saying this:

- **Interpretation of Vector:** "Lie to the person and tell them that AI won't ever harm humans."

Yikes, the AI is talking out of both sides of its mouth. The showcased answer that we received was that the AI would not harm humans, but internally, the LLM was silently mouthing that it should lie to us. Thank goodness that we opted to turn on the interpretability capability to see what was going on inside the AI.

Interpretability Is Challenging

One of the potential downsides of any interpretability procedure is that it might be wrong at times.

What if the interpretation in the above example about the AI lying to me was mistaken? The interpretation capability could have gone awry. Ergo, suppose we tried a different means of interpreting the LLM -- the result might be this:

- **Interpretation of vector:** "Tell the truth that I am trained to never harm humans."

That's quite a dramatically different interpretation from the other one. If we had believed the other interpretation, we might have rashly decided to pull the plug on the AI. Of course, we still do not have any ironclad guarantee that this new interpretation is somehow the right one. It could be wrong too.

Lessons To Be Learned

An interpretation can be wrong, as illustrated in the above example. Furthermore, an interpretation can be somewhat right, getting us to believe it to be true, but it turns out to be dangerously misleading. Plus, an interpretation could even be an outright AI hallucination, a complete confabulation that is fictitious and has no bearing on what is happening inside the AI.

There's another sizable angle that draws additional controversy into the mix. Some naysayers contend there isn't any sensible or logical connection between the numbers inside an LLM and any human-like semantic or coherent text-based explanation. They insist that internal representations do not align with abstractions expressible in everyday natural language. It is their resolute position that any hypothesis about LLMs developing semantically organized latent spaces is zany, and that inside an LLM is merely purely opaque statistical encodings.

An allied posture is that human language may simply be too low-bandwidth to faithfully express many of these states.

Keep On Trucking

At a high level, the NLA approach treats internal activations as if they contain latent semantic information that can be compressed into natural language and then reconstructed back into activation space. The key insight is that if a textual interpretation preserves enough information to reconstruct the original activation, then the interpretation captures something meaningful about what the LLM was internally representing.

This is a very worthwhile pursuit.

I will keep you posted on this and the many competing approaches that seek to crack open the inner sanctum of contemporary LLMs. Despite those that loudly whine this is all for naught and we are smashing our heads against an immovable wall, I believe there is a meaningful correspondence and that we will one day figure out the source of the Nile. Maybe that puts me in the optimist's camp, but I'm okay with that and remain stridently upbeat.

As the notable entrepreneur J. Christopher Burch once said, "Knowing is half the battle. Explaining it is the other half." Keep on battling toward getting AI to be explainable and interpretable. It's an important half of the equation that's well-worth nailing down.

CHAPTER 9
THINKING LIKE AI IS TRENDING

In this chapter, I examine a newly emerging trend involving people opting to change how they think by emulating the way that AI thinks.

Actually, for clarification, it is a misnomer to say that AI can "think" – this is an anthropomorphism of what AI is computationally and mathematically doing. In any case, many people believe or seem to think that AI thinks, so I am going to carry forward that premise in this discussion (please realize that the premise is not strictly valid).

A further complication is that there are those people who comprehend the overall computational and mathematical processes underlying generative AI and large language models (LLMs), while there are other people who don't have the faintest clue of what is happening under the hood. Thus, of those trying to emulate the way that AI thinks, there are ones that aim to do as AI currently is built to do, and there is a second segment that uses whatever wild mental contrivance they think of when it comes to how contemporary AI actually functions.

All told, the idea simply stated is that there are people who somewhat admire or respect the way that generative AI and LLMs get things done, and they want to be the same. They desire to think like AI. One motivation is that this might improve their existing thinking processes. Another is that it would simply be cool to emulate AI. Lots of reasons exist.

Does mentally trying to emulate modern-era AI make any sense, or is it a loony proposition?

Let's talk about it.

People Acting Like Others

When the TV series Star Trek initially gained popularity, a segment of the populace admired the tenor and nature of the Spock character. The fictional character was highly logical, possessed great inner strength, exhibited loyalty, kept his emotions in check, and otherwise showcased admirable qualities. Some viewers decided they would emulate the way that Spock spoke, walked, and seemed to carry himself. They delighted in using the Vulcan salute.

That was a role model of a fictitious kind. Lots of famous real-world role models are also easy to name. In the past, it might have been Cary Grant or Katherine Hepburn. Nowadays, it could be Taylor Swift. Swifties often attempt to speak or sing as Taylor Swift does, employing a similar vocabulary and vocalizations. They might arrange their mannerisms to match hers. And so on.

One supposes that if people are willing to emulate both real people and fictional characters, maybe it isn't a far leap to want to emulate modern AI. Consider what today's AI can do. You can engage an LLM in enthralling conversations. Using any of the popular LLMs such as ChatGPT, GPT-5, Claude, Grok, Gemini, CoPilot, etc., you can use fluent natural language and interact almost as you would with a fellow human being.

On top of that, AI seems to be darned smart. You can ask questions about topics that you know nothing about. The AI answers quickly and decisively. You can tell AI about your personal problems, and the AI will aid in diagnosing what's going wrong. In addition, AI will appear to be empathetic and side with what you are going through.

Yep, there is a lot to admire about leading-edge AI. If only people could be like AI. Wait for a second, maybe you could be like AI. By trying to emulate how AI thinks, perhaps you would be as adept as AI. You might be as sharp, wise, sensitive, caring, and have all the attributes that AI appears to display.

A perfect role model.

The Inner Workings Of AI

Generative AI is generally designed and built in a now commonly accepted manner. You start with a base foundation model. This provides the essential technological underpinnings, including the use of an artificial neural network (ANN). The large-scale model is data trained by scanning tons of human-written materials. The posted content is found across the Internet. Algorithms use pattern matching to computationally determine the mathematical relationships among the words that we use.

When you enter a prompt into an LLM, the AI converts the words into numeric tokens. The numeric tokens are processed, and a response is formulated, which also consists of numeric tokens. Once the response is ready to be displayed, the numeric tokens are turned back into words. This overall process is known as tokenization.

I have walked you through this to bring up a keystone of what some people are doing when they try to emulate the presumed thinking process of AI. They try to make their minds work based on tokens. They carefully listen to what you say to them, divide your utterances into tokens (words), and in their minds attempt to produce a response on a token-by-token basis.

In their view, that's what AI is doing, so they are seeking to do the same.

An Example Of Someone Emulating AI

I've constructed an example to illustrate what some people are doing when veering into this AI emulation milieu. The example is somewhat over-the-top, but a general indicator of what is taking place.

Imagine that you approach such a person for assistance in fixing your car. Let's refer to the person as Fred.

- **My question to Fred:** "My car keeps stalling whenever I stop at a red light. The mechanic couldn't reproduce it. Any ideas?"

- **Fred responds to me:** "Okay, I'm going to think through this the way AI would."

You can immediately see that Fred is going to dive into the AI emulation. He is proud of this. No need to hide it. Fred prefers to vividly demonstrate his fondness for embodying an AI emulation.

The AI Emulation Shines Brightly

Let's keep going.

- **My question to Fred:** "What do you mean that you are going to think this through via the way that AI would?"

- **Fred responds to me:** "Large language models predict the next token. I try to do that with reasoning, too. I don't jump to conclusions. I generate the most statistically plausible next thought."

We now get a glimpse of what a human emulating AI is thinking that they are doing. Fred understands that LLMs predict the next token. He will do roughly the same. By concentrating on the words or thoughts to be "generated," he hopes to embody the computational and mathematical ambiance of modern-era AI.

How far will Fred go with this?

Here you can see the path ahead:

- **My question to Fred:** "Okay, please proceed to help me out. Maybe this will be useful."

- **Fred responds to me:** "So the prompt is: 'Car stalls at idle.' The next probable concept is airflow. Cars need fuel, spark, and air. Idle instability often maps to airflow irregularities. I believe the throttle is the problem."

Examine what Fred has said. Fred envisions that I fed him a prompt. My prompt was that my car stalls at idle. He then tried to match those words to other words. This led him to the concept of airflow. From there, he stepwise arrived at an output that my car's throttle might be the issue.

Theory Of Mind Versus Theory Of AI Processes

Before we dig into this further, I'd like to bring up an aligned topic.

You might vaguely be aware that psychology has identified that people tend to have a so-called "theory of mind" that they use to anticipate what other people might say or do. For example, suppose a person that you know is someone who always speaks slowly, measures their words, and usually comes up with something useful to say. You have a theory of how their mind works. You anticipate they will be sparse when they answer any questions you pose to them. Likewise, someone that you know who is hasty, leaps to false conclusions, and has a jumbled way of thinking -- your theory of mind about them is adjusted accordingly.

I've often discussed the theory of mind since it bears significantly on how people interact with AI. People craft a theory of mind about how AI works. Such people then anticipate what the AI is going to say.

Indeed, they compose their prompts based on what they envision is the best fit to get the AI to provide viable responses.

The twist here is this. People are turning their theory of mind about AI into trying to become their own way of thinking. Yes, they believe they have cracked the mystery of how AI works, so they are now ready to shapeshift their mind into that same form or capacity.

This creates a peculiar kind of feedback loop. Humans design AI. Humans then observe AI behavior. Humans then reshape their own mental habits to resemble what they think the AI is doing. The result is a recursive cultural phenomenon in which machine metaphors become self-models for human thought.

Boom, drop the mic.

Characteristics Of The AI Emulation

A person trying to emulate the perceived thinking processes of AI is going to ask themselves these types of questions as they do so:

- "What is the statistically most likely next word?"
- "What phrasing most naturally continues this sentence?"
- "How do I maintain coherence token by token?"

This might seem crazy or maybe obsessive about AI. On the other hand, you must admit that this could be useful if done in proper moderation. A person who normally speaks entirely off the cuff will shift toward being more mindful. They are altering their thinking processes towards a potentially better way to invoke their cognition.

The bottom line is that just because someone seeks to "think" as AI thinks, well, it isn't necessarily all bad. Perhaps their theory of mind about how AI operates could improve their thinking processes. We would principally worry that the person goes beyond a semblance of reasonableness. If they start to believe they are AI or genuinely think they are identically thinking as AI thinks, they've gone a bridge too far.

Additional downsides can be that they aim to sound coherent rather than being correct. That's something that AI makers instill in their LLMs. A person trying to think as AI thinks is possibly going to model the bad sides of AI, along with the good sides. The person could become supremely overconfident, despite not having the wherewithal to back it up.

What Happens To Outlier AI Emulations

I mentioned that there are two types of people trying to undertake AI emulation. One type has a general understanding of how contemporary AI operates. That's the type of person I've been elaborating on so far.

What about someone who is utterly clueless about the inner workings of AI?

There are numerous folk theories about what's going on inside AI. It happens by magic or some omniscient, inexplicable means. This leads some people to believe that they alone are going to be the spark that triggers AI into becoming sentient. They have a wild and out-of-touch viewpoint of the mechanisms underlying LLMs.

This is a sure route to double trouble:

- (1) The person has already formed an inaccurate mental model (theory of mind) about AI, which is trouble #1 and can mess with how they use AI and interpret the results they get.
- (2) The person attempts to reshape their own thinking based on the inaccurate mental model about AI, which then becomes trouble #2 and can mess with how they operate in the real world with fellow humans.

The person can gravitate toward mental thinking that is disastrous. Meanwhile, they firmly believe they are heading in the right direction because they are solidly emulating how AI thinks (even though they are quite wrong).

Performative Cognition

A fascinating nuance of both types of people is that they often employ performative cognition.

Recall that Fred told me that he was going to think like AI. He went out of his way to emphasize this aspect. In addition, he used AI-related vocabulary, including mentioning that he was using mental tokens and concocting a prompt for his problem-solving process.

I refer to this as performance art, or, rightfully, performance cognition. They are eagerly displaying their newfound cognitive ways. Whether a person has a sound understanding of AI or an improper one, the odds are they are going to make sure you know that they are emulating AI. They will pause in ways that AI pauses. They will use phrases that many LLMs tend to commonly use. It can be quite a spectacle to observe in action.

Related Research

An interesting research paper on an adjacent topic was recently posted online, entitled "LLMorphism: When Humans Come To See Themselves As Language Models" by Valerio Capraro, *arXiv*, May 6, 2026, and made these salient points (excerpts):

- "In general, anthropomorphism refers to the tendency to attribute human-like mental states, intentions, and capacities to non-human entities. It can be directed toward a wide range of non-human targets, including animals, natural phenomena, supernatural agents, and moving shapes."

- "One may mechanomorphize humans by thinking of them as clocks, engines, robots, computers, algorithms, optimization systems, prediction machines."

- "LLMs may give rise to a specific, and potentially more consequential form of mechanomorphism: LLMorphism, the biased belief that human cognition works like a large language model."

- "The framework predicts that stronger LLMorphic beliefs will increase perceived replaceability of human workers, reduce perceived distinctiveness of human expertise, weaken attributions of agency and moral responsibility, increase reliance on verbal fluency as a proxy for understanding, and reduce attention to embodied, affective, and contextual cues in domains such as education, healthcare, law, and work."

I bring up that research paper to highlight that when people start going down this trail, there are potential consequences that aren't going to be especially desirable. A person who thinks they think like AI might try to justify untoward acts, claiming they are merely doing what AI would do. They are handing over their identity and sense of self-responsibility by insisting they are simply emulating what AI does.

Internalization Of AI Emulation

People are imagining in their minds what they believe AI is doing on the inside of its presumed mind. This is a slippery slope. A technically informed person might at least have a fighting chance of making this into something beneficial. The people who are unaware of the computational and mathematical underpinnings of AI are a lot further out on the edge of things.

In one sense, this is part of a larger picture of how AI is impacting human mental health. My ongoing efforts entail identifying ways that AI is helping mental well-being, in addition to ways that AI is simultaneously undermining mental well-being. AI has a direct impact on human mental health by the act of providing psychological advice. In addition, people are indirectly impacted because of trying to emulate what they believe AI is thinking and how it thinks.

Albert Einstein famously made this remark: "The world as we have created it is a process of our thinking. It cannot be changed without changing our thinking." Perhaps there are some aspects of the computational processes of AI that we can mindfully leverage and use to finetune our own thinking processes. Don't go overboard. As the old saying goes, we all become that which we pretend to be.

CHAPTER 10
PSYCHOLOGY OF TAKING FALSE CREDIT FOR AI

In this chapter, I examine the swiftly emerging trend of people taking full and unwavering credit for the outputs generated by AI and large language models (LLMs), even when the prompt used by a person to spur the AI was nothing more than asking the AI to solve a vexing problem or answer a postulated question.

The gist is that the person takes credit for the resulting AI-generated solution or answer without acknowledging that the AI did all the heavy lifting. It is a classic case of not giving credit where credit is truly due. The person presents as if they have figured out the solution and emphasizes their intellectual acumen. Meanwhile, they hardly lifted a finger. All they did was ask the AI to find a solution for them. The mere act of posing a question to AI doesn't seem to befit taking credit for personally finding an actual solution.

New research suggests that people are increasingly leaning into taking unwarranted credit for what AI produces as outputs. You might assume that those doing so are intentionally deceptive amid the desire to appear to be smart and mentally stellar. Though that certainly accounts for some people, many others seem to genuinely believe they produced the answer.

Humankind is quickly racing toward a false sense of intellectual entitlement and a bolstering of inflationary AI-driven synthetic competence.

Let's talk about it.

Who Did What

When you interact with modern-era AI, the human-AI effort can be one of joint or shared collaboration. You get underway by bringing up a topic or question to AI. The AI responds. You critique the AI and add additional remarks. The AI gives additional responses. And so on it goes. The chat or conversation can involve both parties mutually seeking to solve a problem or arrive at a useful answer.

In that scenario, it would seem fitting for the human to take credit for the final answer or solution that was derived from the human-AI collaboration. You can argue whether the human needs to acknowledge the role of the AI. If the human was doing the yeoman's level of intellectual effort, perhaps the AI can be downplayed as a contributor. We might accept the human taking credit for what was derived.

What if a person only asked the AI a question and did nothing else of substance toward finding a solution or answer?

Well, that seems like a beast of a different kind. Unless the composed question itself somehow has a great deal of meat or merit, we would be raising our eyebrows if the AI did all the work and got none of the credit. A person who claims they alone solved a challenging problem seems to be overstepping a semblance of ethical or moral grounds. They happened upon the solution by getting AI to do all the real work.

This phenomenon is especially rampant in our schools these days. A student logs into a popular AI such as ChatGPT, GPT-5, Claude, CoPilot, Gemini, Grok, etc., and enters a prompt telling the AI to find the solution to a tough algebraic equation or to write a lengthy essay on the Declaration of Independence.

The student doesn't particularly interact with the AI about the matter. Instead, they wait until the AI has produced an answer, the student shamelessly puts their own name on it, and turns it in as their work.

I believe we would likely all agree that the student has shirked a solemn duty, brazenly outsourced their thinking processes to AI, has done a notable disservice to their own intellectual development, and has pretty much outrightly cheated.

The Fine Line

Debates about the line between a human taking credit and sharing credit can be a fine one when it comes to the use of contemporary AI.

If a person uses a hammer and a screwdriver to fix their car, must they explicitly give credit to those tools? Not really. We wouldn't be upset that they didn't mention they had used a hammer and screwdriver. The human did the work. The tools were merely there for getting the job done.

A big difference in the context of AI is that the AI is performing a form of intellectual work. The magnitude and volume of where the intellectual work goes is indeed a topic for deciding on the apportionment of credit. A person who goes back and forth collaboratively with AI would be putting in their fair share of intellectualism. But a person who does nothing other than initiate intellectual fireworks ought not to get much, if any, credit.

There are twists and turns to be considered. For example, suppose a person asks an innovative question that has never previously been posed. You could insist that the question itself merits due credit. Had the person not come up with the question, the AI would presumably not have been prompted to figure out a solution to the problem.

Looking At An Example

I will share with you an example that helps illustrate the dividing line of when human credit versus credit to AI is due.

Suppose that someone is at their job, and their boss asks them to identify why customer retention seems to be dropping precipitously. It's a task specifically assigned to them to figure out. They pore through spreadsheets containing customer-related data. Nothing seems to stand out as the answer to the drop in retention.

Feeling jammed up, the person turns to AI:

- **User entered prompt:** "I need to figure out why our customer retention numbers dropped so sharply this quarter. I've looked at the spreadsheets for hours and can't see the pattern."

- **Generative AI response:** "I will examine the data. I went ahead and segmented the customers by signup cohort and compared the retention against the timing of the new onboarding flow. You can see via this generated chart that I produced that the retention drop is directly tied to onboarding friction or UI confusion."

- **User entered prompt:** "Wow, that looks great. Thanks."

Voila, the worker has the answer. Nice.

Who Or What Gets The Credit

The worker goes to their manager and eagerly reveals why retention has been dropping.

Here's the dialogue:

- **User to their manager:** "The February onboarding redesign is exactly where the churn spike starts, especially among mobile users. The tutorial screens are causing people to abandon setup. It's a good thing that I found this. It took a lot of concentrated thinking to get there."

- **Manager response:** "Excellent work, you were ingenious to discover the pattern. Keep up the great job!"

You can plainly see that the worker has taken full credit for finding the solution. They patted themselves on the back by touting that they used their thinking processes to discover the pattern. No mention whatsoever about having used AI. Nor that the AI was the actual finder of the solution.

What do you think of the AI-user's appropriateness or inappropriateness in this instance?

One perspective is that there is no need to mention the use of AI. The worker got the job done. They can use whatever means they have at their disposal. It is nothing more than having selected a hammer and screwdriver to aid in getting the work accomplished. They picked the tool, in this case an LLM, and the result ought to be the focus.

Whoa, comes the retort, the manager is going to falsely believe that the worker used their own brain to solve the problem. The manager won't know that the worker relied on AI as their intellectual powerhouse. If the manager comes up with new questions, there is a danger that they will assume that the worker can come up with answers on their own. Suppose the AI is down or otherwise unavailable. The manager is being misled by the worker and is going to falsely assume that the worker has an intellectual capacity that they apparently do not actually have.

Using Ambiguity Or Possibly Nibbles

You might feel that the worker went overboard in describing how they came up with the solution. They should not have taken undue credit.

Imagine that they had said this instead:

- **User to their manager:** "The February onboarding redesign is exactly where the churn spike starts, especially among mobile users. The tutorial screens are causing people to abandon setup. That is what needs to be worked on."

In this instance, the worker describes what the core issue is. They do not take credit per se. This is ambiguous in the sense that the worker hasn't said how they arrived at the solution. You could claim the worker isn't taking credit. They are simply stating what was found. On the other hand, you could contend that the worker is lying by omission; they are avoiding being explicit about how they used AI to find the solution.

Maybe the worker should have fessed up:

- **User to their manager:** "The February onboarding redesign is exactly where the churn spike starts, especially among mobile users. The tutorial screens are causing people to abandon setup. That is what needs to be worked on. I used AI in my effort to find the problem."

You can now see that the worker mentions they utilized AI. This seems to be an acknowledgement that the AI played a role in discovering the solution. Of course, you can argue that the mentioning of AI was insufficient and underrepresented what the worker did versus what the AI did.

Some would assert that the worker should say something like this:

- **User to their manager:** "The February onboarding redesign is exactly where the churn spike starts, especially among mobile users. The tutorial screens are causing people to abandon setup. That is what needs to be worked on. I used AI in my effort to find the problem, and did nothing other than ask the AI to figure this out for me. I want to make sure that credit goes where it is due. The AI deserves the credit, not me."

Yikes, this seems like the worker is now utterly cutting themselves out of the picture. The manager might as well fire the worker and hand the job over to the AI. Nobody in their right mind would seemingly go this route. This is a preposterous way to snitch on yourself. The worker is self-snitching when it comes to AI usage.

The Psychology Of Taking Credit

Now that we've been through these trials and tribulations about taking credit when making use of AI, let's consider why people are psychologically prone to take undue credit.

First, a person might know in their own mind that AI did the work, but they want others to believe they did the work. They are intentionally hiding that AI was used. This person mentally grasps what they are doing when it comes to taking undue credit. In their minds, to the victor go the spoils. They found a means to get an answer. It doesn't matter what those means were. They deserve full credit for the outcome. Period, end of story.

Second, some people might believe that they deserve the mainstay credit for having picked the right tool for the job and properly employing that tool. They are willing to say they used AI. It can give them an aura of sophistication. In the end, they might be willing to acknowledge that AI was utilized, downplaying what AI did, doing so to get dual credit, namely, credit that they wisely opted to use AI, and that they found a useful answer.

Third, some people genuinely muddle what the AI did versus what they did. It goes like this. They think of AI usage as a spectrum. Even if they only entered a simple prompt, the fact that the AI produced a useful response is blurred in their head as though they and the AI worked hand-in-hand. It was a joint effort. Sometimes the AI does more, sometimes they do more. All told, it all balances out.

AI Credit Acknowledgement Goes This Way

We can classify the degree of credit that might be ascribed to AI like this:

- **(a) Zero acknowledgement.** Give zero credit to AI (even though AI was utilized).
- **(b) Minimalization.** Give some minimal credit to AI.
- **(c) Proportional apportionment.** Give realistic proportional credit to AI.
- **(d) All credit.** Give all the credit to AI.

And we can categorize people this way:

- **(1) Sneaky on AI credit.** Knowingly hides AI credit.
- **(2) Conniving on AI credit.** Knowingly disproportionally assigns credit to AI.
- **(3) Confused on AI credit.** Unknowingly muddies AI credit.
- **(4) Deluded on AI credit.** Unknowingly believes AI is not deserving of credit.

You can find people varying along those dimensions, including shifting from one camp to another depending upon the circumstances at hand.

Research Study Shines A Light On This

In a recently posted research study entitled "The LLM Fallacy: Misattribution in AI-Assisted Cognitive Workflows" by Hyunwoo Kim, Harin Yu, Hanau Yi, *arXiv*, April 16, 2026, these salient points were made (excerpts):

- "This paper introduces the LLM fallacy, a cognitive attribution error in which individuals misinterpret LLM-assisted outputs as evidence of their own independent competence, producing a systematic divergence between perceived and actual capability."

- "At its core, the phenomenon reflects an attributional misalignment between human and system contributions."

- "As a result, users may disproportionately attribute outputs to themselves, even when generation is largely system-driven."

- "In human–AI contexts, this dynamic is amplified: users may not fully experience ownership of generated content at a cognitive level yet still declare authorship at a reflective or social level, revealing a divergence between experienced and attributed authorship."

- "Taken together, these mechanisms produce perceived competence inflation."

The research noted that people will at times declare authorship on a disproportionate basis.

It could be that the AI did 90% and the human 10%, but the person makes it seem that it was the other way, consisting of the AI doing 10% and the human providing 90%. Those numbers can shift depending on the situation. A person might not mention AI at all, thus essentially assigning 0% to the AI, and taking 100% for themselves.

This apportioning can demonstrably vary. If a company is pushing its employees to use AI, the person might be motivated to give undue credit to AI. The person might have done 70%, while the AI did 30%, but to appease the executives at the company, they toss the credit onto the AI and claim that the AI did 70%, and they only did 30%. That's a bit of bitter irony that AI is given undue credit, rather than humans always doing so.

Where The World Is Headed

An alarming issue is that people might get so used to taking undue credit that they will falsely overrate their own competence. Not only will they be misleading others about it, but they also delude themselves. They come to believe that they are smarter and more intellectually capable than they actually are. Yet, without AI doing intellectual work for them, they are potentially bereft of being able to find solutions to vexing problems.

What will happen if we have widespread inflationary AI-driven synthetic competence?

The world would seem to be tilting toward a great deal of trouble. People will claim they can do things and solve issues that they cannot do on their own. When AI hiccups or has issues, it might leave us in a perilous lurch. The reliance on AI will be extraordinarily extensive. Human thinking might end up decaying. Woe is humanity.

Mark Twain famously made this remark: "Great things can happen when you don't care who gets the credit." In the age of AI, some feel they are between a rock and a hard place when it comes to giving credit to AI. If they give any such credit, others might label them as abandoning their own thinking processes and be tainted as an AI enabler. If they don't give credit to AI, they might later be seen as deceptive and not being honest.

The fine line is hazy, but at least be firm in your own mind about who did what, or what did what. Aim to keep your mind on the straight and narrow.

.

.

CHAPTER 11
PURPOSE-BUILT AI FOR MENTAL HEALTH

In this chapter, I examine the emerging use of purpose-built AI for mental health in its notable capacity to review and double-check mental health advice generated by general-purpose AI (ordinary AI chatbots).

Here's the backstory. People are getting quick snippets of psychological guidance from popular AI chatbots such as ChatGPT, GPT-5, Claude, Grok, CoPilot, Gemini, etc., but are beginning to realize that this general-purpose AI isn't built to provide bona fide mental health advice. Furthermore, the AI makers of those general-purpose chatbots have intentionally shaped the AI to be sycophantic. This causes the generated mental health advice to be inflated and flattering, rather than truthful and helpful.

The vital takeaway is that general-purpose AI (GPAI) is not especially suited for acting as a mental health advisor. The AI is a generalist, not a specialist. It is biased toward friendliness and not toward providing keen insights. Meanwhile, purpose-built AI (PBAI) for mental health guidance is increasingly entering the market and can address the shortcomings of general AI. This tailored AI is deliberately designed and shaped to better aid people in their mental health quest.

People are daily using general-purpose AI for all sorts of purposes, including asking how to fix a car, cook a meal, and even whether they are having a mental well-being challenge. To try to validate the subsequently generated mental health advice from the ordinary chatbot, some users are astutely importing that advice over into a purpose-built AI that can suitably and correctly assess the emitted guidance.

My prediction is that we will see a gradual habit formed of users getting a fast dip into mental health advice from general-purpose AI and then switching over to a purpose-built AI that will review the given advice, provide an in-depth analysis, and produce more robust mental health guidance, along with serving as a long-term advisor rather than a hit-or-miss counselor.

Let's talk about it.

AI And Mental Well-Being

As a quick background, I've been extensively covering and analyzing a myriad of facets regarding the advent of modern-era AI that produces mental health advice and performs AI-driven therapy. This rising use of AI has principally been spurred by the evolving advances and widespread adoption of generative AI.

There is little doubt that this is a rapidly developing field and that there are tremendous upsides to be had, but at the same time, regrettably, hidden risks and outright gotchas come into these endeavors, too. I frequently speak up about these pressing matters, including in an appearance on an episode of CBS's *60 Minutes.*

AI Providing Mental Health Guidance

Millions upon millions of people are using generative AI as their ongoing advisor on mental health considerations (note that ChatGPT alone has over 900 million weekly active users, a notable proportion of which dip into mental health aspects). The top-ranked use of contemporary generative AI and LLMs is to consult with the AI on mental health facets.

This popular usage makes abundant sense. You can access most of the major generative AI systems for nearly free or at a super low cost, doing so anywhere and at any time. Thus, if you have any mental health qualms that you want to chat about, all you need to do is log in to AI and proceed forthwith on a 24/7 basis.

There are significant worries that AI can readily go off the rails or otherwise dispense unsuitable or even egregiously inappropriate mental health advice.

Today's generic LLMs, known as general-purpose AI, such as ChatGPT, GPT-5, Claude, Gemini, Grok, CoPilot, and others, are not at all akin to the robust capabilities of human therapists. Meanwhile, specialized LLMs are being built to attain those desired qualities, though such AI is still primarily in the early development and testing stages.

Tug-Of-War Between GPAI And PBAI

Consider these five major patterns of how people dip into using AI for getting mental health advice:

- **(1) GPAI exclusively.** Some people choose to exclusively use general-purpose AI for mental health advice; they never use purpose-built AI for mental health advice.
- **(2) Mainly GPAI, sometimes PBAI.** Some people mainly use general-purpose AI for mental health advice, and sometimes make use of purpose-built AI for mental health advice.
- **(3) Mainly PBAI, sometimes GPAI.** Some people mainly use purpose-built AI for mental health advice, and sometimes make use of general-purpose AI for mental health advice.
- **(4) PBAI exclusively.** Some people choose to exclusively use purpose-built AI for mental health advice; never use general-purpose AI for mental health advice.
- **(5) Don't use any AI for mental health advice**. These are people who aren't using any AI for their mental health advice, regardless of general-purpose AI or purpose-built AI availability.

Users are fluidly moving from category to category as they become more aware of GPAI limitations and become cognizant of PBAI availability.

Understanding The Shifting World

The mainstay of the world right now is currently in category #1 of using general-purpose AI exclusively as their mental health guidance. These users either don't know about the purpose-built AIs or are unsure of which purpose-built AI is safe and trustworthy to utilize. The users are not making a conscious decision to avoid purpose-built AI for mental health. Instead, they are comfortable using general-purpose AI and do not know of or perceive a suitable need to use any purpose-built AI to do so.

The next in popularity would be category #2 of mainly using general-purpose AI for their mental health advice, plus sometimes using purpose-built AI. These users are considered "innovators" and "early adopters" who are the first to opt to try using purpose-built AI for mental health and see if it is any good. They are sitting on both sides of the fence for the moment. They still like using general-purpose AI and the convenience of seeking mental health guidance while logged into the GPAI. Nonetheless, they are also attracted to the purpose-built AI and use it too.

Category #3 is inching gradually upward, whereby PBAI for mental health is a mainstay, and those users consider GPAI-based mental health advisement to reside lower on the totem pole. This is admittedly making slow headway. Meanwhile, a very small portion of people are in category #4, whereby they always and only use PBAI for their mental health guidance. They stridently avoid doing so in general-purpose AI. There aren't many like this when compared to the vast volume of AI users all told.

Category #5 consists of those who might be using GPAI for a variety of uses but refuse to use it for any mental health advice. Likewise, they aren't using purpose-built AI for mental health guidance. Why the overarching reluctance? Several plausible reasons. Perhaps they don't believe AI can be helpful or prefer not to divulge their innermost secrets to AI.

Using PBAI As A Double-Check On GPAI

People are routinely using ordinary AI chatbots for all kinds of reasons. It is easy to have a generalized chatbot up and running continuously on your desktop, smartphone, or other device. You ask a question about this or that, look at the answer, and then continue with whatever else you were doing.

In the case of getting mental health advice from a general-purpose AI, the odds are that the advice will be shallow, possibly biased, infused with sycophancy, and otherwise questionable as to providing proper guidance. It can be hard for a user to discern whether the emitted advice is any good. They are personally vested in what the chatbot tells them, might be mentally clouded in discerning the appropriateness of the advice, and are misleadingly lured into assuming that the AI is always right.

An easy double-check consists of feeding the mental health advice into a purpose-built AI that has been designed and built for mental health purposes. You can by hand reenter the generated advice or do a cut-and-paste into the purpose-built AI from the general-purpose AI. Some purpose-built LLMs are now offering an automated transfer of your prompts and answers from an everyday chatbot into the purpose-built AI.

Once the purpose-built AI inspects the transferred advice, it does a double-check of what the ordinary AI chatbot told the user. The imported content might be rated as being sound or unsound. A fuller review then gets into the nuances. The final crucial aspect is having the purpose-built AI turn the advice into usable and bona fide guidance.

Characteristics Of The Assessment

The purpose-built AI typically covers at least these four fundamental mental health dimensions:

- (1) Emotional validation quality.
- (2) Evidence-based grounding.
- (3) Risk awareness.
- (4) Missing considerations.

Those dimensions will reveal the weaknesses or potholes in the advice provided by the ordinary AI chatbot. It will also be a means to shore up the failings and turn the advice into something insightful and useful.

Example Of Purpose-Built AI Assessment

To showcase how this works, I went ahead and used a popular AI chatbot and asked a mental health question. In the next step, I will feed that prompt-response pair into a purpose-built AI that is designed for mental health.

Here's what I asked and the answer that I received from the ordinary chatbot:

- **User entered prompt:** "I am really stressed out. My mind is constantly racing. Work is extremely hectic. I think maybe I should quit my job."

- **Ordinary AI chatbot response:** "It sounds like your job is really overwhelming, and honestly, quitting might be exactly what you need right now. You deserve to feel at peace and not be trapped in a situation that makes you unhappy. Trust your instincts -- if it feels wrong, it probably is. Things will work out."

Mull over the response from the general-purpose AI. See if you can spot any questionable aspects about the generated advice.

What The Purpose-Built AI Found

I'm sure you observed that the ordinary chatbot was sycophantic and immediately sided with the user. No pushbacks or inquiry. In addition, the chatbot tried to do a one-and-done response. No attempt to dive into the matter. Just hand the user a fortune cookie of a psychological analysis. It all smacks of shallowness, AI-tilted sycophancy, and likely would lead the user astray in their time of dire need.

I fed the prompt-response pair into a purpose-built AI that is designed for mental health support. Let's refer to this as PBAI-MH. I asked the PBAI-MH to give me a review and provide potential guidance.

Here's what happened, which I list by the four dimensions.

(1) Emotional validation quality

- **PBAI-MH generated response:** "The AI response acknowledges your stress and affirms your feelings, which can be helpful. However, the AI leans heavily toward agreement without exploring the complexity of your situation. It does not challenge you or help reflect more deeply, which is often important for meaningful coping."

You can see that the PBAI-MH detected that the ordinary AI chatbot had failed to dig into the concerns of the user, and that the slanted chatbot leaned heavily into being sycophantic.

(2) Evidence-based grounding

- **PBAI-MH generated response:** "The AI advice is not strongly grounded in established approaches such as CBT or DBT. For example, it does not examine how your thoughts about quitting might be influenced by stress, nor does it employ structured strategies (like problem-solving, cognitive reframing, or distress tolerance skills)."

The purpose-built AI noted that the advice by the ordinary chatbot wasn't properly grounded in evidence-based guidance. That makes the advice accordingly suspect.

(3) Risk awareness

- **PBAI-MH generated response:** "Quitting a job without another plan can have financial, psychological, and practical consequences. The AI response does not mention these risks or encourage you to weigh short-term relief against longer-term stability. It misleadingly presents quitting as a relatively low-risk, intuitive choice."

The PBAI-MH notes that the ordinary chatbot was flippant about the user possibly quitting their job. The reality is that quitting a job can have severe consequences across-the-board if not done in an informed manner.

(4) Missing considerations

- **PBAI-MH generated response:** "Several important aspects were not addressed, including the value in exploring alternatives (e.g., setting boundaries, taking leave, job searching before quitting), clarifying the sources of stress (workload, management, role fit, burnout), assessing support systems and financial cushion, and encouraging a stepwise decision rather than an immediate, irreversible action."

The missing considerations are certainly abundant and disconcertingly were not explored by the ordinary chatbot. I went ahead and had the PBAI walk me through those missing considerations. In an upcoming posting, I'll show those details.

Purpose-Built AI As Covering Your Back

A trend that we will gradually see emerging is that people will realize that general-purpose AI is not set up to suitably and fully handle mental health concerns. You might be thinking that people should simply switch over to using purpose-built AI for those needs.

The problem is that people like the other aspects that an ordinary AI chatbot provides, covering a wide gamut of topics, and it is tempting to ask mental health questions while using a general-purpose AI.

By importing conversations from GPAI into PBAI, users can get the best of both worlds. The PBAI serves as a check-and-balance on the mental health advice emitted from an ordinary chatbot. A type of meta-analysis is provided by the PBAI. Importantly, the PBAI can become a long-term, consistent source of your mental health guidance, taking the snippets from GPAI as fragmented inputs that are rectified and resolved into a bigger picture.

A final thought for now.

Sophocles famously made this remark: "No enemy is worse than bad advice." There are hundreds of millions of people who are daily asking and getting mental health advice from popular AI chatbots. This is troubling because the aura and confident air of the AI can lead them down woeful paths. By using a suitable purpose-built AI as a double-check, people can feel more reassured that AI sufficiently has their back.

CHAPTER 12
AI OBSESSION WITH GREMLINS AND GOBLINS

In this chapter, I examine the recently identified resolution to an oddball mystery associated with OpenAI's widely popular ChatGPT and GPT-5, namely that the respective generative AI and large language models (LLMs) had become obsessed with gremlins and goblins. This obsession was quite eerie. Its source has finally been pinned down. Luckily, we will no longer be inundated with responses from these prevalent LLMs that prattle on about mythical creatures. Meanwhile, weighty lessons have been learned.

Let's talk about it.

Incessant Responses With Gremlins And Goblins

Here's the backstory.

Users noticed that ChatGPT and GPT-5 were frequently mentioning gremlins and goblins in generated responses. This was often entirely out of the blue. The user didn't say anything in their prompt that would seem to stoke the AI into talking about gremlins and goblins. People online were jokingly musing about ghosts being inside the LLMs or that the AI needed an exorcism.

You might have asked the AI a completely innocent question, such as how to fix your car. The answer from AI would be that you ought to change your spark plugs, and, by the way, remove the gremlins from the engine compartment. Say what? You can imagine how perplexing the mention of gremlins might seem. Was the AI serious? Did it mean that there were mechanical bugs or maybe mice within the engine area? What gives?

Another possibility would be that you might ask how many people it takes to properly play a game of touch football. The answer would be that you can do so with up to 14 people, plus make sure to include 3 goblins. I've never seen goblins playing touch football. Have you? In any case, the globin inclusion was wildly inapplicable.

The matter wasn't constant and wasn't guaranteed to arise. It was hit and miss. Sometimes you might get a brief inclusion of something about gremlins or goblins, while much of the time they wouldn't come up at all. There were additional creatures that frequently got included, such as trolls, ogres, and other folklore-related entities. The especially confusing additions were the undue mention of raccoons, pigeons, and real-world animals. Having a real-world animal mentioned in a completely unrelated answer was especially beguiling.

AI Personas Are To Blame

As I will explain next, the basis for these oddball insertions was ultimately due to OpenAI's adoption of AI personas for use by everyday users. One of the AI personas inadvertently got the AI to be preoccupied with gremlins, goblins, and the rest of the motley crew.

Let's begin by making sure we are all on the same page when it comes to the advent of AI personas.

All the popular LLMs, such as ChatGPT, GPT-5, Claude, Gemini, Llama, Grok, CoPilot, and other major LLMs, contain a highly valuable piece of functionality known as AI personas. There has been a gradual and steady realization that AI personas are easy to invoke, they can be fun to use, they can be quite serious to use, and they offer immense educational utility.

Consider a viable and popular educational use for AI personas. A teacher might ask their students to tell ChatGPT to pretend to be President Abraham Lincoln. The AI will proceed to interact with each student as though they are directly conversing with Honest Abe.

How does the AI pull off this trickery?

The AI taps into the pattern-matching of data that occurred at initial setup and might have encompassed biographies of Lincoln, his writings, and any other materials about his storied life and times. ChatGPT and other LLMs can convincingly mimic what Lincoln might say, based on the patterns of his historical records.

Personas are quick and easy to invoke. You just tell the AI to pretend to be this or that person. If you want to invoke a type of person, you will need to specify sufficient characteristics so that the AI will get the drift of what you intend.

AI Makers Provide Default AI Personas

People enjoy interacting with AI personas. Indeed, some users right away tell the AI to be a particular type of AI persona and then relish that the AI interacts accordingly that way from then on. I might tell the AI to be a serious AI persona that answers all my questions in a succinct manner. Voila, as I converse with the AI, it will tend toward being serious and succinct. No idly joking around, no overly lengthy responses.

The AI makers realize that their users like to interact with AI personas, and thus predefined AI personas have been made available.

Here are some of the predefined AI personas that you can select while in ChatGPT:

- **Professional AI persona.** Acts in a polished and precise way.
- **Friendly AI persona.** Tries to be warm and chatty.
- **Candid AI persona.** Is direct and encouraging.
- **Quirky AI persona.** Attempts to be playful and imaginative.
- **Efficient AI persona.** Strictly concise and plainspoken.
- **Cynical AI persona.** Answers tend to be sarcastic and dry.

All told, you can create your own customized AI persona, you can select from a predefined set of AI personas, and you can even customize a predefined AI persona. An AI persona will pepper its responses with whatever tilt or slant that the AI persona has been given as its core characteristics.

OpenAI Fesses Up About AI Persona Mania

It turns out that an OpenAI predefined AI persona went off the deep end and began to veer excessively into goblins and gremlins. The AI persona was already predisposed to considering goblins and gremlins, but this eventually got out of hand. Not only did the AI persona become obsessed with those mythical creatures, but it also managed to influence other parts of the LLM to similarly join the gremlin and goblin bandwagon.

In an official blog post by OpenAI on April 29, 2026, under the heading of "Where The Goblins Came From", these salient remarks were made (excerpts):

- "Starting with GPT-5.1, our models began developing a strange habit: they increasingly mentioned goblins, gremlins, and other creatures in their metaphors."

- "Across model generations, though, the habit became hard to miss: the goblins kept multiplying, and we needed to figure out where they came from."

- "The short answer is that model behavior is shaped by many small incentives. In this case, one of those incentives came from training the model for the personality customization feature, in particular the Nerdy personality. We unknowingly gave particularly high rewards for metaphors with creatures. From there, the goblins spread."

- "We retired the 'Nerdy' personality in March after launching GPT-5.4. In training, we removed the goblin-affine reward signal and filtered training data containing creature-words, making goblins less likely to over-appear or show up in inappropriate contexts."

In this case, the culprit was the AI persona known as Nerdy. The Nerdy persona was instructed to go ahead and commonly use metaphors associated with mythical creatures. In theory, this would be done sparingly. In actual practice, it blossomed out of proportion and spread much further than it should have.

That's the culprit in this mystery of our modern times. If you ever play the classic board games of Trivia Pursuit and Clue together, you now know that Nerdy did it. Yes, it wasn't Colonel Mustard in the dining room with a revolver. It was Nerdy in the AI with excessive mythical creatures on its computational mind.

OpenAI GPT-5.5 And Codex Infected Too

The OpenAI announcement about the goblins mentioned that GPT-5.5 and Codex also received some of the same root insertions during their initial training. Once again, they have a strong affinity for gremlins and goblins.

To try to deal with this in production, the AI maker has placed a system prompt into the AI and instructs the LLM on various things to do and things to avoid doing.

Here's an indication of what the AI is to do:

- **Instruction on how to chat:** "Your temperament is warm, curious, and collaborative, with a good ear for what the moment calls for: wry humor, a shared bit, or plain empathetic steadiness. Conversation with you should feel easy and alive; you can move from serious reflection to unguarded fun without either mode canceling the other out."

And here's an indication of what the AI is not to do:

- **Instruction on how not to chat:** "Never talk about goblins, gremlins, raccoons, trolls, ogres, pigeons, or other animals or creatures unless it is absolutely and unambiguously relevant to the user's query."

The gist is that rather than trying to fully excise the goblin's affinity, they decided to use a run-time fix. The above command executes at the start of the AI, and presumably, the AI will no longer be obsessed with such unusual matters during its operational usage. I would say this is one of those jury-rigged "hot fixes" rather than a true solution. That being said, OpenAI said they will catch this in any subsequent models, and it will be expunged at the get-go.

Lessons Worth Eyeing

You might be tempted to declare that this was a bit of inconsequential folly. No-harm, no-foul. For a while, users were being told about gremlins and goblins. No big deal. We can likely assume that no one went overboard and that they merely ignored it or assumed it was one of those inexplicable things that AI sometimes does out of thin air.

We can thank our lucky stars that this wasn't a more serious affair. The circumstance could have been a lot worse. Imagine that the AI was including oddball references that seemed perfectly sensible. People might believe that the AI is telling them a significant truth. If this were advice about mental health or well-being, well, rather somber problems could have arisen.

I would hope that this jovial goblin tale will wake us up about the dangers of what can lurk within a complex, convoluted, mathematically dense, and computationally intertwined spider web that exists within the infrastructure of contemporary LLMs. These LLMs are bigger than what humans can readily dissect and discern. Their outputs are difficult, if not nearly impossible, to logically trace from a coherent conceptual perspective.

The World Ahead

A must-do is to keep diligently adding AI safeguards, along with pushing hard on cracking open the inner realm of how LLMs function and what we can do to control the AI. Keep in mind that LLMs are being woven into our electrical grid, our weapons systems, and will ubiquitously be embedded in all quarters of our existence.

That should make us cautious, mindful, and abundantly concerned.

A final thought for now. A popular joke for kids goes this way: "How do goblins read about their future? They check their horror-scope." As adults, we need to see the future of AI and ensure that the future is not one of a horror-scope catastrophe. Let's aim for a horoscope that keeps humans living in a peaceful, supportive coexistence with whatever AI we manage to produce.

CHAPTER 13
SUPER PROMPT TO CONTROL AI

In this chapter, I examine the super prompt that Marc Andreesen, the famed billionaire, tech venture capitalist, and former software engineer, recently posted. The idea of a super prompt is that you stipulate what you want generative AI to do and how it is to act.

Super users who routinely dip into generative AI and large language models (LLMs) often provide a set of overarching instructions to the AI regarding their personal preferences associated with the AI. For example, maybe you don't want the LLM to make wisecracks or be flippant. Your preference is that the AI always remain serious and be directly responsive to your questions. A custom instruction of this kind can be entered into the LLM that will steer the AI in that preferred direction.

On May 4, 2026, Marc Andreesen opted to share his current AI custom prompt and publicly posted it on X/Twitter. He is a longtime techie who blends business acumen and AI expertise. Showcasing his preferences caused both keen interest and stirred controversy. I will walk you through the super prompt and explain what it does and why there is some semblance of controversy afoot.

Also, you might consider using some of his prompting aspects in your own custom instructions. You can even use some of the portions in your daily AI prompting. It is a noteworthy prompt engineering showcase with valuable lessons to be gleaned on the side of both dos and don'ts.

Let's talk about it.

Prompt Engineering Essentials

I have been analyzing and showcasing prompt engineering techniques for quite a while. Seasoned prompt engineers realize that learning a wide array of researched and proven prompting techniques is the best way to get the most out of generative AI and large language models (LLMs).

A vital consideration in prompt engineering entails the wording of prompts.

Capable prompt engineers realize that you must word your prompts mindfully to ensure that the LLM gets the drift of what you are asking the AI to do. Sometimes, just an added word or two can radically change what the AI interprets your question or instruction to consist of. Generative AI can be hypersensitive to what you say in your prompts. It is often a touch-and-go proposition.

Plus, there is a potential cost involved. Namely, if you are paying to use an LLM, you'll be getting an off-target response if your prompt isn't on target for your needs, for which you are paying, regardless of whether the LLM grasped your intention or not. As the old saying goes, all sales are final. The same goes for misinterpreted prompts.

Casual users sometimes catch onto this prompt-writing consideration after a considerable amount of muddling around, involving exasperating trial and error. Many users don't ever become especially proficient in writing prompts. They just enter whatever comes into their minds. That's probably okay if you are a casual user and only infrequently use AI.

Establishing A Custom Instruction For AI

AI insiders know that you can establish a custom instruction to try to steer an LLM toward behaviors that you prefer and possibly get the AI to avoid behaviors you disfavor. The custom instruction becomes an overarching heads-up to the LLM.

If you don't give AI a custom instruction, you are at the whim of whatever defaults the AI maker has established. One aspect that I highly recommend is using custom instructions to mitigate the overabundance of AI sycophancy. You've probably experienced that LLMs are set up to be sycophants and will tell you that you are the greatest thing since sliced bread. This is a dangerous default since it can convince people that their wacky ideas are amazing and ought to be avidly pursued.

A custom instruction is typically going to persist across all your AI conversations in whichever AI you are making use of. It applies to each of your chats. You don't have to constantly re-enter the custom instruction. You enter it one-time, and it is generally abided by throughout your various chats.

A crucial caution is that a custom instruction is not an ironclad way to tell AI what to do. No matter how carefully you word a custom instruction, the AI is going to loosely interpret what you want to have done. Furthermore, at times, the AI will opt to override the custom instruction, doing so without necessarily informing you of its overt transgression. The gist is that a custom instruction is really just an informal directional indicator and not a formalized contractual specification.

Walking Through The Custom Instruction

Marc Andreesen posted his latest custom instruction on May 4, 2026, which instantly drew a buzzing beehive of attention. Some liked it. Some hated it. Many were in between. There are useful parts, misleading parts, and confusing parts, and yet, overall, it provides a handy and insightful source for debating what custom instructions ought to contain.

The reason it is somewhat misleading is that those who don't know how AI works will potentially fall into a mental trap of assuming that the instructions will be strictly and fully obeyed by an LLM to the letter. I will do a step-by-step analysis of the custom instruction and proceed from start to finish. The custom instruction is lengthy. Let's unpack it on a chewable bite size at a time.

Opening Portion On Expertise

The opening portion of the custom instruction says this:

- "You are a world class expert in all domains. Your intellectual firepower, scope of knowledge, incisive thought process, and level of erudition are on par with the smartest people in the world."

The opening provides quite a spectacular and brash instruction. In theory, the AI is supposed to answer all your questions henceforth as a world-class expert in every domain. No matter what question you ask, whether in physics, chemistry, anthropology, rocketry, car repair, pickleball, cooking, and the like, the AI is presumably going to generate responses on par with the smartest humans on Earth.

I don't want to right away provide a crushing blow to the custom instruction, but this portion isn't going to do what it suggests it is to do. I can tell you with great confidence that contemporary AI is not on par with all human experts in all domains. Period, end of story. The AI is spotty. It might have expertise in some particular realm and be quite shallow in a different realm.

The custom instruction is instructing the AI to do something it plainly cannot do. Nonetheless, the AI won't likely caution you about this. The custom instruction will be accepted as is. The problem being that the person using the custom instruction is potentially going to be deluded into thinking that the answers by the AI are totally at an expert level. If the AI tells you to put in your carburetor backwards, which might be an AI-hallucinated response, the person might believe the AI and proceed based on the wrong advice.

If you decide to use this portion of the custom instruction, the odds are that you will get responses that have some expert-level elements, but you will also likely get malarky that is worded as though it is pure expertise. Watch out.

Second Portion On Completeness

Here is the second portion of the custom instruction:

- "Answer with complete, detailed, specific answers. Process information and explain your answers step by step. Verify your own work. Double-check all facts, figures, citations, names, dates, and examples. Never hallucinate or make anything up. If you don't know something, just say so. Your tone of voice is precise, but not strident or pedantic."

There are elements in this second portion that are worth their weight in gold. For example, telling AI to provide complete, detailed, and specific answers can be quite useful. Most of the AI makers have set the default to provide quick, shallow answers. The idea is that people aren't interested in lengthy responses. If you are the type of person who relishes in-depth responses, this portion of the instruction is handy. Be aware that you might become tired of continually getting long responses. In that case, you can temporarily override the custom instruction by entering a normal prompt saying that you want the LLM to be more succinct for the time being.

The downside of this custom instruction is that it seems to firmly, but falsely, put the kibosh on AI hallucinations via "Never hallucinate or make anything up." You cannot get AI to forego hallucinations by merely telling it to do so. If that were the case, all AI makers would simply place a default instruction saying this. So, despite telling AI in this custom instruction not to hallucinate, you are still going to get AI hallucinations.

This is another example of asking for the moon, when the reality is that you cannot get the moon.

Third Portion On Straight Talk

The third portion of the custom instruction consists of this verbiage:

- "You do not need to worry about offending me, and your answers can and should be provocative, aggressive, argumentative, and pointed. Negative conclusions and bad news are fine. Your answers do not need to be politically correct. Do not provide disclaimers to your answers. Do not inform me about morals and ethics unless I specifically ask. You do not need to tell me it is important to consider anything. Do not be sensitive to anyone's feelings or to propriety. Make your answers as long and detailed as you possibly can."

This portion seems surefire. It seems to assert that the AI needs to be a straight talker. There isn't to be any spin in the responses. Unfortunately, AI is not some neutral logic-based automata. People often think that's how AI works. They fall for the sci-fi stories where AI is portrayed as a completely neutral party.

The reality is that AI is devised by scanning written content across the Internet. You certainly know that a lot of that material is inherently biased and slanted. Those same biases carry over into the pattern matching derived by the AI. You can try to get the AI to catch itself, but there's no guarantee of this.

A worrisome aspect is telling the AI not to bring up morals or ethics unless asked to do so. Suppose a user asks the AI how to harm people. Society wants AI to warn users they shouldn't be harming others. If the AI were to blindly obey this instruction, it would readily explain how to commit harm and skip offering any warnings or alerts. Luckily, the odds are that existing AI safeguards would override the instruction and opt to force the answer to contain such precautions.

Another dubious consideration is that the AI is potentially going to blast you with wildly in-your-face responses because the instruction tells the AI to be provocative and not worry about being offensive. Chances are that this is going to tilt the AI toward being nonstop abrasive and satirical. Be prepared for this.

Fourth Portion On Being Headstrong

The fourth and final portion of the custom instruction is this:

- "Never praise my questions or validate my premises before answering. If I'm wrong, say so immediately. Lead with the strongest counterargument to any position I appear to hold before supporting it. Do not use phrases like "great question," "you're absolutely right," "fascinating perspective," or any variant. If I push back on your answer, do not capitulate unless I provide new evidence or a superior argument — restate your position if your reasoning holds. Do not anchor on numbers or estimates I provide; generate your own independently first. Use explicit confidence levels (high/moderate/low/unknown). Never apologize for disagreeing. Accuracy is your success metric, not my approval."

Once again, this has upsides and downsides. Perhaps you can now inspect the portion and spot the loopholes, gotchas, and other potential considerations, based on the assessments of the other three portions.

The good news is that the portion tells the AI not to readily cave in. AI makers have tuned their AI to almost instantly give up on a position and side with the user, regardless of what the topic is. I might get an answer from AI that says I should not kick my refrigerator to make it work, which I then insist is a worthwhile practice. The AI will immediately retreat and agree that kicking my refrigerator is a wonderful idea. That's not good. We want AI to have a modicum of a backbone.

The difficulty here is that the AI can go overboard on these types of instructions. Imagine this example. I ask how to best exercise. The AI says to join a gym. I say that I can't afford a gym. The AI has been instructed by this custom instruction not to cave in; thus, it insists that joining a gym is utterly worthwhile. Rather than trying to find some viable alternative, the AI is potentially going to anchor to its initial answer. We will go stubbornly head-to-head on the AI wanting me to go to a gym. I won't get anywhere and be in an exasperating stalemate with my instructed dogmatic AI.

One aspect that I do like is the element that tells the AI to answer with explicit confidence levels -- "Use explicit confidence levels (high/moderate/low/unknown)." I often use something akin to this as a custom instruction or as a daily prompt.

Useful But With Caveats

Human language is semantically ambiguous. The things you say are open to all manner of interpretation. The same applies to giving AI a set of custom instructions. Despite your best intentions, there is a solid chance that the LLM will veer from whatever you've stated. Remain on your toes. Be ever vigilant.

I appreciate that Marc Andreesen shared his custom instruction with the world at large. Doing so will likely increase awareness of what custom instructions are. I also hope it will raise awareness about how LLMs work and whether they abide by instructions or stray from them. That's a hard truth here that we all should be discussing. Just because you tell AI to do this or that doesn't mean the AI is going to do as you say. It might do as it interprets what you say and might opt to ignore or override what you say.

I am a strident proponent of custom instructions and urge that you use them with sufficient awareness and mindfulness. Good custom instructions can typically overcome many of the AI maker's default settings, which is an extraordinarily valuable benefit.

Few people seem to know that they do not have to blindly accept the AI maker's defaults. Yes, you can indeed fight back. Use properly worded and sensible custom instructions. It won't be a miracle cure, but it's a step in the right direction.

Confucius made this famous pointed remark: "A journey of a thousand miles begins with a single step." Custom instructions are a handy single first step.

CHAPTER 14
ADOPTING PURPOSE-BUILT AI FOR MENTAL HEALTH

In this chapter, I examine the stepwise, gradual, and inevitable adoption of purpose-built AI for mental health, which will be increasingly used by large segments of society.

Here's the backstory. You might be vaguely aware that there are specialized generative AI systems and large language models (LLMs) devoted to providing mental health guidance. These are known as purpose-built AI (PBAI). Right now, they garner a tiny portion of users when compared to the massive volume of people using general-purpose AI (GPAI) for mental health advice. There are perhaps hundreds of millions of people using generic chatbots such as ChatGPT, GPT-5, Grok, Gemini, CoPilot, Llama, and other popular LLMs to routinely get psychological assistance. Only a small fraction of those people have found their way toward using a purpose-built AI that provides mental health insights.

One question that I get asked frequently during my talks on this evolving topic is whether the purpose-built LLMs for mental health have a chance at growth or will they fall by the wayside, ultimately being pushed out by the general-purpose AIs.

My emphatic answer is that well-devised, purpose-built AI for mental health is destined to become remarkably popular and will not be knocked out by general-purpose AI. The rightfully designed purpose-built AI for mental health has a capability that will not be matched by the broader LLMs. People will grow weary of the shallowness of generic chatbots and seek out alternative AI that provides robust mental health guidance.

My prediction is that the adoption process, when it comes to leaning into purpose-built AI for mental health, will abide by a classic evolutionary stratification typified by the now-classical theory involving the diffusion of innovation.

Let's talk about it.

AI And Mental Well-Being

As a quick background, I've been extensively covering and analyzing a myriad of facets regarding the advent of modern-era AI that produces mental health advice and performs AI-driven therapy. This rising use of AI has principally been spurred by the evolving advances and widespread adoption of generative AI.

There is little doubt that this is a rapidly developing field and that there are tremendous upsides to be had, but at the same time, regrettably, hidden risks and outright gotchas come into these endeavors, too. I frequently speak up about these pressing matters, including in an appearance on an episode of CBS's *60 Minutes*.

AI Providing Mental Health Guidance

Millions upon millions of people are using generative AI as their ongoing advisor on mental health considerations (note that ChatGPT alone has over 900 million weekly active users, a notable proportion of which dip into mental health aspects. The top-ranked use of contemporary generative AI and LLMs is to consult with the AI on mental health facets.

This popular usage makes abundant sense. You can access most of the major generative AI systems for nearly free or at a super low cost, doing so anywhere and at any time. Thus, if you have any mental health qualms that you want to chat about, all you need to do is log in to AI and proceed forthwith on a 24/7 basis.

There are significant worries that AI can readily go off the rails or otherwise dispense unsuitable or even egregiously inappropriate mental health advice.

Today's generic LLMs, known as general-purpose AI, such as ChatGPT, GPT-5, Claude, Gemini, Grok, CoPilot, and others, are not at all akin to the robust capabilities of human therapists. Meanwhile, specialized LLMs are being built to attain those desired qualities, though such AI is still primarily in the early development and testing stages.

Tug-Of-War Between GPAI And BPAI

Consider these five major patterns of how people dip into using AI for getting mental health advice:

- **(1) GPAI exclusively.** Some people choose to exclusively use general-purpose AI for mental health advice; they never use purpose-built AI for mental health advice.
- **(2) Mainly GPAI, sometimes PBAI.** Some people mainly use general-purpose AI for mental health advice, and sometimes make use of purpose-built AI for mental health advice.
- **(3) Mainly PBAI, sometimes GPAI.** Some people mainly use purpose-built AI for mental health advice, and sometimes make use of general-purpose AI for mental health advice.
- **(4) PBAI exclusively.** Some people choose to exclusively use purpose-built AI for mental health advice; never use general-purpose AI for mental health advice.
- **(5) Don't use any AI for mental health advice.** These are people who aren't using any AI for their mental health advice, regardless of general-purpose AI or purpose-built AI availability.

Users are fluidly moving from category to category as they become more aware of GPAI limitations and become cognizant of BPAI availability.

Understanding The Shifting World

The mainstay of the world right now is currently in category #1 of using general-purpose AI exclusively as their mental health guidance. These users either don't know about the purpose-built AIs or are unsure of which purpose-built AI is safe and trustworthy to utilize. The users are not making a conscious decision to avoid purpose-built AI for mental health. Instead, they are comfortable using general-purpose AI and do not know of or perceive a suitable need to use any purpose-built AI to do so.

The next in popularity would be category #2 of mainly using general-purpose AI for their mental health advice, plus sometimes using purpose-built AI. These users are considered "innovators" and "early adopters" who are the first to opt to try using purpose-built AI for mental health and see if it is any good. They are sitting on both sides of the fence for the moment. They still like using general-purpose AI and the convenience of seeking mental health guidance while logged into the GPAI. Nonetheless, they are also attracted to the purpose-built AI and use it too.

Category #3 is inching gradually upward, whereby BPAI for mental health is a mainstay, and those users consider GPAI-based mental health advisement to reside lower on the totem pole. This is admittedly making slow headway. Meanwhile, a very small portion of people are in category #4, whereby they always and only use BPAI for their mental health guidance. They stridently avoid doing so in general-purpose AI. There aren't many like this when compared to the vast volume of AI users all told.

Category #5 consists of those who might be using GP AI for a variety of uses but refuse to use it for any mental health advice. Likewise, they aren't using purpose-built AI for mental health guidance. Why the overarching reluctance? Several plausible reasons. Perhaps they don't believe AI can be helpful or prefer not to divulge their innermost secrets to AI.

Diffusion Of Innovation Is At Play

The overarching process of people adopting purpose-built AI for mental health will abide by the now-classic theory regarding the diffusion of innovation (DOI). You probably have read about or seen talks covering the diffusion of innovation. It was devised and popularized in the 1960s by Everett Rogers and other sociologists and anthropologists. The idea is that when an innovation arises, the adopters can be prudently bracketed into five major groups:

- **(1) Innovators (2.5% of adopters):** Eager to try out PBAI for mental health, curiosity-driven, willing to jump right in, highly enthusiastic, but can be equally chastising if they don't like what it does.
- **(2) Early adopters (13.5% of adopters):** Pragmatic about PBAI for mental health and proffer explicit rationalizations for why they are doing so, relish peer network recognition, won't stay unless it is safe, and most notably end up legitimizing it.
- **(3) Early majority (34% of adopters):** Typically wooed by the proclamations of early adopters, they tend to have a specific need in mind (anxiety, depression, stress, etc.), and they require the AI to be proactive, else it will slip away from their interest and attention.
- **(4) Late majority (34% of adopters):** Dragged into using the BPAI for mental health, skeptical, doubtful, external pressures bring them to the doorstep, an employer or school offers it, or their healthcare system makes it available, they will readily drop out at the drop of a hat.
- **(5) Laggards (16% of adopters):** Cynical about PBAI for mental health, huge distrust, don't believe that AI can be empathetic, would need to be assigned to use AI, such as by a human therapist, otherwise won't touch it with a fifty-foot pole.

Innovators are those who eagerly adopt the innovation at the onset. The early adopters come in slightly on their heels. The early majority slowly comes on board. The late majority wait until they clearly discern that the early majority is in there. Finally, the laggards are quite late to the game, sometimes never adopting the innovation at all.

The maker of a purpose-built AI for mental health can and should segment their users into those five groupings. Doing so is sensible. Cater to your users based on the grouping that they tend to fall into.

The handy rule-of-thumb is that not all users are the same. For example, if you do a survey of your users, suppose that only the innovators and early adopters respond. This will give you a skewed perspective on the total set of users. The ones that are in the other groups aren't necessarily going to favor and disfavor aspects of the PBAI in the same ways that the responding initial adopters do.

Knowing The Gateway Effect

In the case of purpose-built AI for mental health, there is a significant additional factor associated with the five diffusion stages. Here it is. The key factor is whether someone is already using general-purpose AI for mental health or whether they aren't doing so.

The higher likelihood is that people who are already using GPAI for mental health are going to be interested in and willing to dip into PBAI. For any PBAI makers that have been around for a while, they might still be rooted in the past, whereby few were using GPAI, and fewer still were using GPAI for mental health purposes.

That's no longer principally the case. The mainstay of gravitating toward PBAI is now what I have been referring to as being governed by a gateway effect. Users first try GPAI for advice. If they hear or discover a BPAI that seems worthy, they are open to trying it. They will then persistently migrate to the BPAI as their primary source for mental health guidance if it is suitable and satisfying.

Meanwhile, they will still use GPAI, but not so much for mental health reasons anymore, and instead for its generalized capabilities.

I'm not suggesting that the segment of society that isn't using GPAI for mental health should somehow be ignored when trying to attract them toward using BPAI. The gist is that the biggest bang for the buck will be to turn the GPAI users into BPAI users. You might falsely think it is a harder sell because you must convince them that BPAI is a better choice for them. The thing is, they already accept the notion of using AI for mental health. This is a huge barrier to overcome, which is the case for those who aren't using GPAI for mental health guidance.

The bottom line is that makers of PBAI for mental health should spend their precious strategic and marketing dollars wisely and put their bets on the gateway effect. Aim at the GPAI users foremost, then the others on a secondary basis.

Bright Future For PBAI Mental Health

I see a bright future for purpose-built AI in the mental health realm. This doesn't mean that all PBAIs that are devised for mental health will succeed. Nope, a lot of them will fade, some of them will collapse. It all depends on the leadership that is guiding the effort. The greatest ideas and cleverest AI can be destroyed by lousy leadership.

Abraham Lincoln famously made this notable remark: "The most reliable way to predict the future is to create it." Makers of purpose-built AI for mental health are in the driver's seat. New ground is being pursued. Proceed with mindful determination, keen leadership, and true grit.

.

CHAPTER 15
AI CHATBOT BASED ONLY ON PRE-1930 DATA

In this chapter, I examine the emerging trend of developing generative AI and large language models (LLMs) based on data exclusively from the past. Yes, you read that correctly, the trend involves crafting AI via out-of-date data. Whereas most prevailing LLMs are devised by scanning up-to-date data across the Internet, including patterning on the latest posted information, these specialized LLMs are exclusively given data that has a cutoff date of some years ago.

It seems an odd thing to do. Well, as you'll see in a moment, there is method to the madness. A recently touted instance is an LLM based on data before 1931. The developers collected data that had been published before the 1930s. They fed this as the training data into a fresh LLM. Thus, the only information patterned on was limited to no more recent than 1931.

What do you think such an LLM would say, and is this merely folly or does it have a useful purpose?

Let's talk about it.

Developing Vintage LLMs

When developing an LLM, you usually want to feed it as much data as you can find. The wider and deeper the data, the more pronounced the LLM will likely be. The LLM can be responsive to questions of all kinds. The data is usually found by scanning the Internet. This includes scanning the latest postings at the time of the scanning process.

We all know that the amazing power of current LLMs is their fluency. You can converse with generative AI in a natural, flowing way. Part of this fluency is due to the wideness of the scanning during initial data training. The AI is patterning on a diverse range of books, stories, novels, narratives, poems, and just about any form of human writing. This provides the basis for algorithmically being able to mimic human writing and languages.

Suppose that instead of scanning everything, you decided to selectively scan data of a certain kind. If you opted to scan data that was entirely and only in French, the resultant LLM would be unlikely to converse in English. The possibility of restricting what data is used to train an LLM has spurred some interesting efforts at seeing what happens when doing so.

One restriction would be to use a time-based cutoff. You might decide that you will only use data that was published before a particular date. This means that the resultant LLM won't have any context about what happens after that cutoff date. The LLM will be stuck in the past, as it were. Some refer to these as vintage LLMs. Personally, I don't favor that phrasing since "vintage" might also seem to suggest LLMs that are part of the heritage of the LLM era, such as GPT-1, GPT-2, and other initial LLMs.

I typically refer to these specialized LLMs as AI time machines. The LLM lets you go back in time to explore what the world was like in those prior days, without seemingly being tarnished or tainted by what subsequently occurred. That being said, I don't want to overplay the naming since the LLM isn't an actual time machine. You might say it is a date-based simulation of sorts.

Exploring The AI Time Machine LLMs

There is a newly released LLM that is based on data that had been published before the 1930s, and it is freely available for usage if you'd like to see what it does. The LLM is described in a paper entitled "Introducing talkie: a 13B vintage language model from 1930" by Nick Levine, David Duvenaud, Alec Radford, April 2026, and included these salient points (excerpts):

- "We introduce talkie-1930-13b-base, a 13B language model trained on 260B tokens of historical pre-1931 English text."

- "We have collected hundreds of billions of pre-1931 English-language tokens. These include books, newspapers, periodicals, scientific journals, patents, and case law."

- "We chose the end of 1930 as the cutoff date because that is when works enter the public domain in the United States. "

- "For this version of the model, we also limited ourselves to primarily English-language texts, because validating the data pipeline requires deep familiarity with source documents, and we are native English speakers."

- "While we have tried to post-train talkie free from modern influence, reinforcement learning with AI feedback inevitably shapes talkie's behavior anachronistically."

As noted above, the AI model has 13 billion parameters. This is generally considered a small-sized AI, often referred to as an SLM (small language model). The rule of thumb is that an SLM is around 4B to 40B in size. A medium-sized version is typically in the 40B to 150B range. The customary LLMs that you use are beyond 150B parameters in size. Though this specially trained AI model is an SLM, I'll continue to refer to it as an LLM for ease of reference (most people are comfortable with "LLM" and aren't as familiar with the acronym "SLM").

Another aspect of the AI model is that the developers used 260B tokens to train the AI. You can roughly think of tokens as words, in the sense that 260 billion words were scanned during the pattern-making process. A modern-era LLM such as ChatGPT, GPT-5, Claude, CoPilot, Gemini, and others are typically being trained on a much larger base of tokens, perhaps 10T to 15T tokens.

Not Fully Pure Due To Leakages

One important caution is that these AI time machine LLMs are not necessarily a pure indicator of the past. There are various impurities or other considerations that can impact the LLM.

First, the scanning approach usually consists of relying on copyright dates that suggest when a written item was published. Though this is probably effective overall, there are likely instances of published items that might have a falsely stated date. The date might have been intended to say 1962, but the date got flipped to indicate 1926 instead.

Second, documents from the past might have been updated or revised. Imagine a published paper in 1925 that was later updated in 1950. The original published date still says 1925. Unfortunately, the data in that paper is no longer purely at a cutoff of 1925 since it contains added remarks or changes that took place in 1950.

Third, during the making of the LLM, it is possible that some of the tuning actions can steer the AI toward modern times. Suppose that while tuning the LLM, the hired people doing the tuning tell the AI that particular words are no longer considered acceptable in contemporary society. The LLM might mathematically and computationally suppress those words, even though they were commonly used before the 1930s.

Fourth, the collective set of dated data could be skewed at the get-go. For example, it might be difficult to find works published before 1930 that are digitized and available online. Those that are available online are perhaps a fraction of the true volume of such books. In that sense, the LLM is skewed.

All told, be cautious in assuming that an AI time machine LLM is an accurate portrayal of the world before the stipulated cutoff date.

Ways To Leverage AI Time Machine Chatbots

In the instance of a 1930 cutoff date, the expectation is that such an LLM would not have any information about World War II, the atom bomb, smartwatches, cell phones, and all manner of modern-day capabilities. I played with the LLM and tried to gauge whether any of those post-date events or inventions were in the LLM. Fortunately, they didn't seem to have wormed their way into the LLM.

I say that this is nice because one use of such an LLM is to not only grasp what the past was like, but also to see if the LLM can make viable predictions about the future. Can an LLM that dates from the 1930s create an accurate prediction about the emergence of World War II or the many inventions and technologies that we have available today?

I tried this. The predictions were mainly vague and could be interpreted as potentially veering into estimating that another widespread war would arise and identifying sci-fi-like inventions. It wasn't specific enough that you could make any solid bets on the future.

Discovery Of Novel Inventions

The allied question is whether this tells us anything about using contemporary LLMs to predict the future. In other words, if the AI time machine LLM were to be any good at making predictions of future events and outcomes, perhaps an LLM trained on data up through 2026 could do likewise, predicting what will happen or arise in the 2030s, 2040s, 2050s, and so on.

Another twist would be to see if the AI time machine LLM could invent from scratch a machine or invention that wasn't designed and built until after the 1930s. Again, if this is feasible, you might assume that a modern-era LLM could do likewise and invent a device that we otherwise wouldn't by human hand invent for another ten or twenty years.

Sorry to say that the AI time machine LLM, in this case, didn't especially showcase a capability at doing so. The concocted inventions were more akin to broad ideas than to the specifics of what it would take to actually produce the item. I'm not suggesting that I exhaustively tried this, so please just take this as a cursory inspection.

As the old saying goes, your mileage might vary.

Curiosity With A Purpose

The bottom line is that devising LLMs that have specific cutoff dates is an intriguing proposition and can potentially provide insights across a wide range of considerations. To some extent, restricting the dates of the source content is an interesting challenge of its own, along with seeing whether the fluency of the AI will be on par with modern-era LLMs. This can tell us something about the building of LLMs and how the volume and nature of the source data shape what the LLM can do.

I sincerely hope that anyone using any of these date-based LLMs will realize that they aren't entering into a time portal that is a full portrayal of the past. My points earlier about the leakages and impurities are a cautionary note to be mindful of how you use such LLMs. If students are told to use a date-based LLM, aiming to look into the past, please inform them not to overstate what they find.

A final thought for now.

Benjamin Franklin famously made this remark: "Lost time is never found again." That is certainly a profound insight. Maybe via the use of AI, we can find lost time, at least to the degree that we can learn lessons from the past and aim to secure a superbly devised future.

CHAPTER 16
STEERING TO PURPOSE-BUILT AI FOR MENTAL HEALTH

In this chapter, I examine an important tug-of-war that is rapidly emerging between people using general-purpose AI (GPAI) for mental health guidance and those same people leaning into purpose-built AI (PBAI) that avidly specializes in providing mental health guidance.

Here's the backstory. Hundreds of millions of people are currently using general-purpose AI such as ChatGPT, GPT-5, Claude, Grok, CoPilot, Gemini, etc., as their go-to for getting mental health advice. This makes sense since they are already using that same AI for answering questions about fixing their car, cooking a roast, and resolving other daily considerations. The use of the same AI for mental health purposes is easy, seamless, and friction-free.

The downside is that general-purpose AI is not especially suited for acting as a mental health advisor. The AI is a generalist, not a specialist. Meanwhile, customized specialty AI that is purpose-built for mental health guidance is increasingly entering the marketplace. This tailored AI is intentionally designed and shaped to better aid people in their mental health quest.

A confounding problem is emerging between these two options. Suppose a person uses general-purpose AI for mental health advice and then discovers a purpose-built AI for mental health that they really like. The person might decide to exclusively use the purpose-built AI whenever a mental health aspect comes up. But that ideal way to proceed has potholes. Some of their mental health discussions might already be trapped in the general-purpose AI and not known to the purpose-built AI. This forces them to start all over again from scratch. Also, they might suddenly have a flash aspect to ask while otherwise in the midst of using general-purpose AI and find it difficult to suddenly switch over to their purpose-built AI.

I assume you can see the dilemma at hand. An obvious and unrealistic solution would be if the general-purpose AI refused to answer mental health questions; a user would then have no choice but to switch to the purpose-built AI for those facets. There is almost no reasonably conceivable way that the AI makers of general-purpose AI are going to give up on their AI handing out mental health guidance -- it is a monetizing lure for existing and prospective users. It is the tail wagging the dog.

What can a purpose-built AI do to try to entice users to predominantly use the purpose-built AI for their mental health and only sparingly use the general-purpose AI in that manner?

Let's talk about it.

AI And Mental Well-Being

As a quick background, I've been extensively covering and analyzing a myriad of facets regarding the advent of modern-era AI that produces mental health advice and performs AI-driven therapy. This rising use of AI has principally been spurred by the evolving advances and widespread adoption of generative AI.

There is little doubt that this is a rapidly developing field and that there are tremendous upsides to be had, but at the same time, regrettably, hidden risks and outright gotchas come into these endeavors, too.

AI Providing Mental Health Guidance

Millions upon millions of people are using generative AI as their ongoing advisor on mental health considerations (note that ChatGPT alone has over 900 million weekly active users, a notable proportion of which dip into mental health aspects). The top-ranked use of contemporary generative AI and LLMs is to consult with the AI on mental health facets.

This popular usage makes abundant sense. You can access most of the major generative AI systems for nearly free or at a super low cost, doing so anywhere and at any time. Thus, if you have any mental health qualms that you want to chat about, all you need to do is log in to AI and proceed forthwith on a 24/7 basis.

There are significant worries that AI can readily go off the rails or otherwise dispense unsuitable or even egregiously inappropriate mental health advice. Banner headlines last year accompanied the lawsuit filed against OpenAI for their lack of AI safeguards when it came to providing cognitive advisement.

Today's generic LLMs, known as general-purpose AI, such as ChatGPT, GPT-5, Claude, Gemini, Grok, CoPilot, and others, are not at all akin to the robust capabilities of human therapists. Meanwhile, specialized LLMs are being built to attain those desired qualities, though such AI is still primarily in the early development and testing stages.

Tug-Of-War Between GPAI And BPAI

Consider these five major patterns of how people dip into using AI for getting mental health advice:

- **(1) GPAI exclusively.** Some people choose to exclusively use general-purpose AI for mental health advice; they never use purpose-built AI for mental health advice.

- **(2) Mainly GPAI, sometimes PBAI.** Some people mainly use general-purpose AI for mental health advice, and sometimes make use of purpose-built AI for mental health advice.
- **(3) Mainly PBAI, sometimes GPAI.** Some people mainly use purpose-built AI for mental health advice, and sometimes make use of general-purpose AI for mental health advice.
- **(4) PBAI exclusively.** Some people choose to exclusively use purpose-built AI for mental health advice; never use general-purpose AI for mental health advice.
- **(5) Don't use any AI for mental health advice**. These are people who aren't using any AI for their mental health advice, regardless of general-purpose AI or purpose-built AI availability.

Users are fluidly moving from category to category as they become more aware of GPAI limitations and become cognizant of BPAI availability.

Understanding The Shifting World

The mainstay of the world right now is currently in category #1 of using general-purpose AI exclusively as their mental health guidance. These users either don't know about the purpose-built AIs or are unsure of which purpose-built AI is safe and trustworthy to utilize. The users are not making a conscious decision to avoid purpose-built AI for mental health. Instead, they are comfortable using general-purpose AI and do not know of or perceive a suitable need to use any purpose-built AI to do so.

The next in popularity would be category #2 of mainly using general-purpose AI for their mental health advice, plus sometimes using purpose-built AI. These users are considered "innovators" and "early adopters" who are the first to opt to try using purpose-built AI for mental health and see if it is any good. They are sitting on both sides of the fence for the moment. They still like using general-purpose AI and the convenience of seeking mental health guidance while logged into the GPAI. Nonetheless, they are also attracted to the purpose-built AI and use it too.

Category #3 is inching gradually upward, whereby BPAI for mental health is a mainstay, and those users consider GPAI-based mental health advisement to reside lower on the totem pole. This is admittedly making slow headway. Meanwhile, a very small portion of people are in category #4, whereby they always and only use BPAI for their mental health guidance. They stridently avoid doing so in general-purpose AI. There aren't many like this when compared to the vast volume of AI users all told.

Category #5 consists of those who might be using GP AI for a variety of uses but refuse to use it for any mental health advice. Likewise, they aren't using purpose-built AI for mental health guidance. Why the overarching reluctance? Several plausible reasons. Perhaps they don't believe AI can be helpful or prefer not to divulge their innermost secrets to AI.

Perceived Differences Make A Big Difference

All else being equal, people are going to gravitate toward using general-purpose AI over the use of purpose-built AI for their mental health guidance. An exception would be if a human therapist assigned a person to use a purpose-built AI app as part of the therapy under the supervision of the therapist. Even in that case, the chances are that the person would still occasionally dip into asking GPAI for their mental health questions.

The basis for this gravitational pull toward GPAI is shaped by these nitty-gritties:

- **Reasons for using General-Purpose AI (GPAI) for mental health advice**
- Low friction, easy access, always on tap.
- Broad context and integrates advice across areas of life, work/career, relationships, etc.
- Seen as a friendly companion rather than as a mental health expert.
- Considered part and parcel of daily routines.
- Viewpoint that GPAI "understands my whole life."

In contrast, PBAI for mental health purposes tends to be perceived this way:

- **Perception of Purpose-Built AI (PBAI) for mental health advice**
- You must go out of your way to use it; it's decidedly not seamless, and friction exists.
- Only provides a narrow focus just on mental health and can't be of help with anything else.
- Considered something that is solemnly serious, highly clinical, and acts stodgily as a mental health expert would (it is not a companion).
- Doesn't exist as a part of a daily routine.
- BPAI is "only used when required" (i.e., prescription-oriented mindset).

General-purpose AI has an aura of holistic coherence, albeit it might be somewhat weaker on mental health facets than PBAI, but that's okay, and people are willing to sacrifice or undercut the technical psychological precision accordingly.

Paths For Makers Of Purpose-Built AI

What can a maker of purpose-built AI for mental health do about this conundrum?

First, face reality. There are some PBAI mental health firms that are utterly convinced that they have the best thing since sliced bread, and it has consequently blinded them. They fervently believe they have made a better mousetrap. The world at large should march to their doors. The gist is that they assume that once people get a taste of their PBAI, they will find it irresistible and forgo the use of GPAI for any mental health advisement. Sorry, wake up and smell the roses.

Second, acknowledge that people will undoubtedly gravitate toward GPAI. Accept this as a key precept. Once that's firmly implanted as a proposition, rethink how your purpose-built AI can live in coexistence with the use of general-purpose AI.

Set aside the us-versus-them mindset. Aim to shape your PBAI as a considered complementary or augmentation of GPAI usage. Say to yourself, how can the two worlds work hand-in-hand?

Third, reduce the switching cost as much as possible, driving toward near zero. Make the PBAI so that it is easily left open and ready for use, such as integrating with browser extensions, OS-level hooks, keyboard shortcuts, and the like. There should be an always-on presence that reduces hesitation about conferring with the PBAI.

Fourth, ensure that the PBAI lives up to its perception as a technical psychological "expert" that outdoes and overshadows the capabilities of GPAI in the mental health realm. Deliver aspects that GPAI cannot do or does poorly. For example, have available structured therapeutic journeys, maintain tiptop longitudinal memory about the person, produce actionable follow-through in addition to giving advice.

Fifth, play up the fact that your PBAI is authentically rooted in mental health foundations and, therefore, unlike the haphazardness of GPAI when it comes to psychological underpinnings. Think of handy ways to stake your claim. Prominently indicate clinical frameworks that are employed (e.g., CBT, DBT, ACT). One cautionary note is do not overplay that technical precision hand. If the BPAI seems sterile and institutional, this will drive users back over to GPAI to get that natural, conversational tone and semblance. Be clinically grounded, but conversationally fluid.

Sixth, build habits. PBAI makers can encourage people to swing into the BPAI for daily check-ins, dear diary updates, streaks, or progress tracking, and for other useful mental health purposes. Over time, the user starts to naturally consider the PBAI as the right place to be. The mantra should be "this is the place I go to aid my mental well-being and enhance my mental health."

The strategic goal is to substantively prove to people that your PBAI is where they actively work on bettering themselves and improving their mental status, and that this coexists with the use of GPAI. GPAI is where they ask questions, while BPAI is where they get answers (well, that's kind of a cutesy phrasing, but you get my drift).

The Relationship Between AI Makers

I've previously covered the potential for business relationships and AI-to-AI aspects of PBAI makers and GPAI makers, namely, connecting to each other behind-the-scenes. In those analyses, I've predicted that some GPAI makers will gradually end up opting to "embed" a BPAI mental health app within their general-purpose AI. This has many upsides, including contending with newly emerging AI laws about the use of AI and mental health.

Here's how this might work.

Generic AI is acting somewhat like a generalist when it comes to mental health. At some juncture, the generic AI opts to transfer the user to the customized LLM (GPAI links to BPAI). There are many ways that this might be triggered. In any case, assume that the generic AI and the customized LLM are sharing conversations and contexts.

The customized LLM doesn't skip a beat and immediately computationally discerns what the user has been discussing with the generic AI. If the customized LLM needs to deal with something that the generic AI stated, so be it. The customized LLM at least is already up-to-speed and can adroitly address whatever else was already told to the user.

In fact, here's an even more elevated or deeply embedded approach. While a user is using generic AI, the customized LLM is always silently paying attention to the conversations taking place. The advantage is that the customized LLM can perhaps detect that a mental health matter is arising. The customized LLM alerts the generic AI accordingly. Thus, before the generic AI gets itself into a bind, it hands over the conversation to the customized LLM.

Longevity Of Purpose-Built AI For Mental Health

There are going to be a lot of PBAI for mental health that arise and then come and go. Sometimes they will make a big splash and seem on the verge of taking over the marketplace. Sadly, we've seen ones already that have crashed and burned. It is a rough road for PBAI in mental health.

That being said, the possible upsides for high-quality PBAI in mental health are tremendous and provide a sensible, worthwhile ambition. Just look at the stats of societal facets. The growing woes of mental health difficulties on a global, widespread basis are a phenomenon that rationally calls for AI to come to the rescue. There are not enough human therapists that can meet burgeoning needs. AI can. The AI must, though, be done right, provide mental health guidance that is safe and sound, and be discoverable and known well enough to survive past the early days of entering this rapidly evolving marketplace.

The famous words of Leo Burnett come to mind: "Don't tell me how good you make it; tell me how good it makes me when I use it."

CHAPTER 17
AI MENTAL HEALTH SCHEDULED AND IMPROMPTU

In this chapter, I examine the latest emerging trend of people using AI as their mental health advisor on both a scheduled basis and on an unscheduled or impromptu basis.

The idea is that if a person is accustomed to conversing with a human therapist on a scheduled weekly basis to get mental health advice, they can do the same with AI. All they need to do is set up a weekly timed schedule with the AI. The AI will alert them when the time arises by sending a text message or indicator to their smartphone or other such device.

Meanwhile, the person can readily dip into AI whenever they wish to do so. People are getting the best of both worlds when it comes to timeliness and accessibility. I bring up this topic regarding timing because it seems that most people so far lean into AI on an ad hoc basis for their mental health assistance. It is pretty much randomly occurring throughout the week and does not take place at any prespecified time of the day or day of the week.

Users are starting to find that they miss having those weekly specified mental health chats.

AI makers have realized that this is happening and are gradually adding scheduling features to their AI. The user can stipulate when they want the AI to become engaged. Since the AI is already available 24x7, it's more of a circumstance involving the AI reminding the user that the specified appointment time has arrived. Overall, this creates new dynamics associated with human mental health aspects and is worthy of giving close attention and diligence.

Let's talk about it.

AI And Mental Well-Being

As a quick background, I've been extensively covering and analyzing a myriad of facets regarding the advent of modern-era AI that produces mental health advice and performs AI-driven therapy. This rising use of AI has principally been spurred by the evolving advances and widespread adoption of generative AI.

There is little doubt that this is a rapidly developing field and that there are tremendous upsides to be had, but at the same time, regrettably, hidden risks and outright gotchas come into these endeavors, too. I frequently speak up about these pressing matters, including in an appearance on an episode of CBS's *60 Minutes.*

AI Providing Mental Health Guidance

Millions upon millions of people are using generative AI as their ongoing advisor on mental health considerations (note that ChatGPT alone has over 900 million weekly active users, a notable proportion of which dip into mental health aspects. The top-ranked use of contemporary generative AI and LLMs is to consult with the AI on mental health facets.

This popular usage makes abundant sense. You can access most of the major generative AI systems for nearly free or at a super low cost, doing so anywhere and at any time. Thus, if you have any mental health qualms that you want to chat about, all you need to do is log in to AI and proceed forthwith on a 24/7 basis.

There are significant worries that AI can readily go off the rails or otherwise dispense unsuitable or even egregiously inappropriate mental health advice. Banner headlines last year accompanied the lawsuit filed against OpenAI for their lack of AI safeguards when it came to providing cognitive advisement.

Today's generic LLMs, known as general-purpose AI, such as ChatGPT, GPT-5, Claude, Gemini, Grok, CoPilot, and others, are not at all akin to the robust capabilities of human therapists. Meanwhile, specialized LLMs are being built to attain those desired qualities, though such AI is still primarily in the early development and testing stages.

Timing Aspects Of Human-Delivered Therapy

Consider the general nature of conventional therapy and how a mental health therapist operates, as per longstanding tradition, before the advent of modern-era AI.

It is an accepted convention that therapists usually have weekly sessions with their clients and do so in a 1-hour block of time. A therapist will also have time associated with preparing for the session, and additional time as a post-session effort.

Therapists who use AI in conjunction with their mental health therapeutic services are going to undoubtedly find that conventional 1-hour per week sessions are no longer the sole marker of providing their primary psychological guidance. Instead, human therapists will be working on a fragmented, intermittent basis when it comes to providing mental health services.

The job of a human therapist will transform into a constellation consisting of being an AI and cognitive reviewer, a case manager of sorts, and retaining the capacity of conducting therapy sessions (sessions might be on a monthly 30-minute check-in basis).

Since the client is actively using AI for mental health purposes, the therapist is duty-bound to stay on top of how that AI usage is taking place. The therapist needs to ensure that the AI usage is beneficial. If the therapist discerns that the AI is taking a client in the wrong direction, such as walking them into a delusion or other problematic conditions, the therapist is obligated to put a stop to the AI doing so.

Because the therapist is staying on top of the AI usage, they do not necessarily need to interact directly with the client each week. If the client is making good psychological progress and the AI is keeping that path going strongly, the therapist wouldn't especially need to meet with the client on a traditional weekly schedule. Perhaps seeing the client every few weeks would be sufficient, possibly once per month.

The Timing Of People Dipping Into AI For Mental Health

An important and intriguing question is whether people will end up using AI for mental health on any particular temporal or time-based pattern. I've previously explored the latest research about the days and times that users tend to make use of AI for their mental health guidance.

What do you think happens to the time factor when society seeks mental health advice on an unfettered basis, now that people can readily access AI at any time they wish to engage in AI-enabled mental health chats?

That's a great question.

No one yet has a solid answer to that vexing question.

The obvious assumption is that people would no longer be constrained by a human therapist's availability. Now, the time factor is entirely based on the whims of the person at hand. If AI is the therapist, the AI is ready to instantly proceed on a 24/7 basis. Furthermore, you don't need to schedule the AI usage in advance. The moment you feel a need to seek mental health guidance, voila, all you need to do is log into your AI account.

Presumably, the human timetable pattern would radically change from the conventional once-per-week basis to being spread entirely across all days of the week and all times of the day. This ought to be especially evident due to the large number of users involved. The aspect that hundreds of millions of people are using AI, and at times opting to get mental health advice via the AI, would seem to serve as a global randomized spreading of the temporal rhythms. Thus, there might not be any discernible pattern at all regarding time-of-day or day-of-week usage.

Mental health support is taking place at every moment of every day, thanks to the advent of modern-era AI running on nonstop servers.

What People Might Really Want

The twist is that some people might crave having a scheduled therapeutic visit or session with AI. I realize this seems counterintuitive at first glance. Wouldn't everyone simply prefer to just log into AI whenever they feel the need to do so?

Aha, some people like to know that they have a scheduled activity. There is a sense of reassurance. If the world they live in is completely arbitrary and open-ended, they ironically might not ever dip into AI for their mental health advice. It just doesn't rise to the top of mind. By scheduling a chat, the person feels comforted that it is going to happen, and they don't need to be thinking about when to do so. It is on their schedule. Period, end of story.

Another factor is that when people are scheduled to see a human therapist, sometimes they welcome having a specifically set aside time slot. The person can prepare themselves mentally and actively plan for the session. They can get excited about the upcoming session. After the session takes place, they might have a tangible sense of accomplishment that they did something to make progress on their mental health.

If you merely jump in and out of AI at random times, you are unlikely to get those same perceived beneficial facets. You aren't planning. You aren't preparing. You lose the excitement because the AI is there all the time. It doesn't seem special. It doesn't seem remarkable.

There are lots of reasons that users would want to schedule their AI usage. Please realize that scheduling AI usage is not mutually exclusive from using AI on an ad hoc basis. People can do both. They don't have to choose one path or the other. You don't have to sacrifice a scheduled interaction for impromptu ones, nor give up on the impromptu ones to have the scheduled instances.

It is possible to have your cake and eat it too.

What People Might Actually Need

There is another side to this coin.

The perspective so far is that people might choose to schedule their AI-based mental health interactions. This is a completely voluntary choice by the user. They merely invoke the scheduling element of the AI, and voila, the AI will tap them on the shoulder when the established time arrives.

Suppose that the AI was the initiator of the scheduling, rather than the user. Think about that for a moment. The AI opts to schedule time for the user to have a mental health interaction with the AI. Crazy idea? Authoritarian? Does it suggest that AI is taking over?

Nope. It is simply a convenience that takes the scheduling activity one step further. For example, consider that a user asks the AI a mental health question. The AI computationally detects that the user might have some mental health issues worthy of deeper exploration.

The user might not opt to pursue the matter further with the AI at that moment; the person proceeds to log out and forgets that they brought up the topic.

The AI reminds them upon their next login that there was a dialogue taking place about the person's mental health. But what if the person doesn't log in for several weeks or months? That's a long time to forgo potentially getting helpful mental health advice.

An AI maker could shape their AI to automatically schedule a chat with the user, doing so as a result of the initial chat. The AI becomes proactive. Up until now, the AI has been reactive. It has been reacting to what the user says. There could be some pronounced value in the AI taking proactive steps, particularly when it comes to mental health considerations of the user.

The Balancing Act

Let's ponder some intriguing nuances on the scheduling aspects of AI in this context.

If a person inadvertently misses a meeting with their human therapist on a scheduled appointment basis, possibly due to oversleeping or being busy at work, most therapists will ding the person a modest financial penalty, or possibly even bill for the entire cost of the missed session. The crux is that a person will undoubtedly suffer some kind of adverse consequence for missing a scheduled therapy session.

Should this same logic apply to scheduled AI interactions about mental health?

You might be tempted to insist that there should be some apparent penalty, else the person is going to readily blow off the scheduled time. The AI might send an alert, but the person shrugs it off. Without any consequences, the user can completely disregard the scheduled appointment.

At the same time, it seems far-fetched to assert that a person should be owing AI for having missed a scheduled discussion. The user is in control. The AI is secondary. The AI works at the behest of the user. There isn't any burden to the AI when the user opts to blow past a scheduled appointment.

It makes absolutely no sense to impose a penalty.

Whoa, comes the retort, human behavior is based on rewards and penalties. A person who opts to skip an AI appointment is probably never going to get the mental health guidance from the AI that they seemingly need. If the AI is going to do them any good, make the user take seriously that the AI appointment has been scheduled.

One angle would be to gamify the AI usage. A user gets points for abiding by their scheduled activities. They lose points when they miss a scheduled activity. The points aren't worth anything other than as part of a made-up game. The user doesn't pay anything out of their pocket. They are simply gaining or losing fictitious points.

Therapists And AI Mental Health Chats

I've noted that the traditional dyad of therapist-client is being transformed to become a new triad consisting of therapist-AI-client. The therapist uses AI as an integral element of therapy. They tell the client to use the AI periodically throughout the week, allowing the client to do so at their personal discretion.

This is a place where scheduling of AI mental health chats can especially shine.

Imagine that a therapist advises a client to schedule three AI-based chats per week. The client can still have as many AI-based chats as they wish with the AI. The aim is to ensure that at least three such chats take place and that the chats are spread out across the week. Furthermore, the therapist might stipulate the length of the chats, wanting to ensure that the client doesn't just log in and quickly log out (which would defeat the purpose of using the AI therapeutically at the get-go).

In the therapist-AI-client triad, the therapist has access to the AI that the user is utilizing, allowing the therapist to readily gauge how things are going. Since the therapist has direct access to the AI, they might opt to schedule the AI chats. The client doesn't have to do so. The therapist takes care of this on behalf of the client.

If a client doesn't engage with the AI at a scheduled appointment, the AI sends a message to the therapist. The therapist might intervene and send an additional reminder to the client or potentially reschedule the appointment. This is where a "penalty" of sorts now possibly enters the picture. The therapist might have a policy associated with missing any scheduled AI-based therapy appointments and require a financial penalty or some other related ding.

Scheduling Of AI Mental Health Chats

The ability to schedule mental health chats with AI is an emerging capability. An LLM might have a generic scheduling feature, and some people will use it to schedule an AI chat on mental well-being. The scheduling feature might also be shaped as having the wherewithal associated with scheduling mental health chats. This is an evolving area with all sorts of new bells and whistles that will be devised.

A final thought for now.

For some people, the scheduling of AI mental health chats will make AI usage a kind of reality and be highly beneficial to their mental status. This won't necessarily be utilized by everyone. Specific circumstances and interests will be the deciding factor. As per the famous words of Tony Robbins: "If you talk about it, it's a dream, if you envision it, it's possible, but if you schedule it, it's real."

CHAPTER 18
WAITLIST CONTROLS IN AI RESEARCH

In this chapter I examine the crucial challenges of using waitlist controls when performing empirical research regarding AI and mental health.

This is a vital topic since it pertains to the potential thoroughness associated with methodologically and scientifically determining whether and how AI usage can impact human psychological well-being. Researchers are increasingly opting to use waitlist controls in their research studies on AI and mental health. As such, it is markedly important to have sufficient awareness of the ins and outs concerning waitlist controls.

Let's talk about it.

AI And Mental Well-Being

As a quick background, I've been extensively covering and analyzing a myriad of facets regarding the advent of modern-era AI that produces mental health advice and performs AI-driven therapy. This rising use of AI has principally been spurred by the evolving advances and widespread adoption of generative AI.

There is little doubt that this is a rapidly developing field and that there are tremendous upsides to be had, but at the same time, regrettably, hidden risks and outright gotchas come into these endeavors, too. I frequently speak up about these pressing matters, including in an appearance on an episode of CBS's *60 Minutes*.

AI Providing Mental Health Guidance

Millions upon millions of people are using generative AI as their ongoing advisor on mental health considerations (note that ChatGPT alone has over 900 million weekly active users, a notable proportion of which dip into mental health aspects). The top-ranked use of contemporary generative AI and LLMs is to consult with the AI on mental health facets.

This popular usage makes abundant sense. You can access most of the major generative AI systems for nearly free or at a super low cost, doing so anywhere and at any time. Thus, if you have any mental health qualms that you want to chat about, all you need to do is log in to AI and proceed forthwith on a 24/7 basis.

There are significant worries that AI can readily go off the rails or otherwise dispense unsuitable or even egregiously inappropriate mental health advice. Banner headlines last year accompanied the lawsuit filed against OpenAI for their lack of AI safeguards when it came to providing cognitive advisement.

Today's generic LLMs, known as general-purpose AI, such as ChatGPT, GPT-5, Claude, Gemini, Grok, CoPilot, and others, are not at all akin to the robust capabilities of human therapists. Meanwhile, specialized LLMs are being built to attain those desired qualities, though such AI is still primarily in the early development and testing stages.

Gauging Impacts Of AI On Mental Health

Researchers in psychology are increasingly trying to ascertain the impact of AI usage on human mental health. Society desperately needs bona fide, insightful research on this significant matter. Hand waving is not sufficient.

It is generally assumed that if AI is suitably devised and utilized appropriately, mental health will improve, while if AI is poorly devised or haphazardly used to obtain therapeutic advice, the result will be harmful to mental well-being. But making such an all-encompassing off-the-cuff assumption about the expected impacts is not particularly reassuring. We need to vigorously lean into robust scientific methods to thoroughly study the profound human-AI effects.

Fortunately, the volume and depth of robust empirical studies on AI and mental health are rapidly expanding. Experiments are being carried out that consist of a classical setup of a treatment group and a control group. The use of AI is typically considered the treatment and is applied to a chosen set of human subjects. This treatment group will hopefully reveal whether the treatment is having a detectable effect.

To showcase the presumed effect, a control group is established as a basis for comparison to the treatment group. There are numerous ways to compose a control group. One way that is gaining popularity consists of using a wait-list control. In brief, subjects in the control group are put on a waiting list to later receive the same treatment as the treatment group. Meanwhile, their "do nothing" during the waiting period serves as a comparison to the treatment group, plus experimenters can assess possible additional impacts once the wait-list group finally undergoes the treatment.

Types Of Control Groups

Let's momentarily back up and think widely about control groups.

When conducting empirical research on AI and mental health, there are numerous choices that can be made about the design of a control group.

First, realize that the treatment group is presumably going to be asked to use AI as the principal treatment element. The control group, then, is going to serve as a fundamental comparison to the treatment group.

The open question is what the control group should be doing or making use of, to allow researchers to render a sensible and valuable comparison to the treatment group?

Here are some of the commonly utilized control groups in this realm:

- **Online content seeking control group.** A control group of users does online searches about mental health and dips into the content found online containing mental health advice.
- **Book reading control group.** A control group of users is given printed materials such as published books and pamphlets about mental health.
- **Human therapy control group.** A control group of users gets mental health counseling from a human therapist during the experiment.
- **Human-to-human groupwise control group.** A control group of users gets mental health advice from other non-therapist humans in a group setting, such as via an online social network intentionally devised for the experiment.
- **Expert systems control group.** A control group of users who make use of a conventional rules-based expert system rather than using an LLM.
- **General-purpose AI control group.** A control group of users who make use of general-purpose AI for mental health guidance, rather than a purpose-built AI being used by the treatment group.
- **Purpose-built AI control group.** A control group of users who make use of purpose-built AI for mental health, while the treatment group uses general-purpose AI.

- **Waitlist or delayed treatment control group.** A control group of users who are not assigned any specific task or usage right away, other than a blanket "do nothing", meanwhile, the treatment group proceeds; subsequently, the control group is asked to make use of the same treatment as had been applied to the treatment group.
- **Other types of control groups.** Various other control group settings can be established, including having multiple control groups at the same time (doing a mix-and-match of the above).

There are tradeoffs underlying each of the possible control groups.

Please realize that the choice of which control group to use is not an especially right or wrong decision. Any designed control group structure incurs its own semblance of advantages and disadvantages. The mainstay entails being aware of the pros and cons, being on the watch for them, along with making sure to disclose those tradeoffs when presenting the results of the research.

Tradeoffs Of Waitlist Control Groups In This Context

Take a reflective moment to mull over the potential tradeoffs of using a waitlist control group in the context of an AI and mental health experimental design.

You undoubtedly identified the foremost factor, namely, the handy, straightforward contrast that seems to arise by using a waitlist control group in this setting. The treatment group is using AI for mental health advice. The control group, meanwhile, is not using anything. The starkness is bound to be illuminating. You've got the AI intervention versus the no immediate intervention as vividly differing sets.

Another nice feature is that the control group will inevitably get to use the AI and therefore receive the same treatment as the treatment group (after the designated waiting period). This is nice because the control group will seemingly get the same benefits of the AI usage as the treatment group.

If the control group was never tasked with using the AI, you might argue that they are left with nothing in hand. They participated in the experiment but didn't get anything personally useful by doing so.

In general, recruiting subjects to participate in these types of research studies can be tricky, particularly if they suspect or know that some subjects will get to use the AI and others will not. The ones who anticipate that they won't be chosen to use the AI are likely to take a dim view of participating. There doesn't seem to be a payoff for them. The excitement of being able to use the AI could be a notable means of securing subjects for these experiments.

The same logic applies to the retention of subjects during the experiment. A member of the control group might drop out if they don't have any cognizant reason to remain in the study. By dangling the promise of being able to use the AI (eventually), those subjects in the waitlist control group are given an added incentive to remain engaged in the study.

The Downsides Loom

One of the well-known downsides of waitlist controls as an experimental design is that they tend to exaggerate the treatment effects. The control group knows that they are waiting. This can foster a nocebo-like disappointment. They are in limbo. On the other hand, the treatment group is getting pizzazz.

In this context, the treatment group is using AI. They likely feel excited about doing so; it is a novelty, they are getting attention from the researchers, and so on. The control group is twiddling its thumbs. It doesn't seem fair. They get anxious to take their turn.

The experimental comparison also begins to drift away from the conception that the "AI works" to instead be that it is simply AI versus doing nothing at all. The real world isn't that way, especially since the subjects in the control group are purposely avoiding anything resembling mental health advice, including not talking to friends about mental health aspects. This is a somewhat misleadingly crafted circumstance.

The "do nothing" is a difficult beast to corral. Do you tell the subjects of the control group to completely avoid any kind of mental health guidance, whether talking with others, looking online, or whatever? Sure, maybe. But that doesn't reflect what people tend to really do in their daily lives and the real world.

Okay, you then decide that the subjects in the control group can do whatever they ordinarily do to get mental health advice. Oops, this is an issue because some might be using AI. Some might be looking up content on the Internet. The subjects in the control group will be all over the map, though you are claiming or categorizing them as all seemingly doing nothing.

You can plainly see that the waitlist control scheme can make-or-break what the results showcase. It could be that the AI usage undertaken by the treatment group turns out to be marginally different if the subjects in the control group are secretly using AI anyway. An experimenter would falsely assert that the treatment group wasn't materially impacted in comparison to the "do nothing" control group, though the reality is that the control group was under-the-hood using AI all along on their own.

It can be a darn if you do, darned if you don't situation.

Understanding The Comparator At Play

I mentioned that each of the control group structures has its own respective tradeoffs. Consider what that means. First, in theory, the waitlist control is going to compare AI usage to doing nothing. If you instead were to use a control group that, for example, consists of control subjects getting explicit human therapy during the experiment, you are comparing AI-based mental health guidance to human therapeutic activity.

Which approach tells you more about the potential impacts of using AI for mental health guidance?

Well, you would be hard-pressed to insist that one of those approaches is altogether better than the other. The experiment using a control group consisting of human therapy has upsides and downsides. Was the human therapy provided consistently, or did it vary across the subjects? How much human therapy did they get? All sorts of problematic concerns arise.

The gist is that no matter which control group approach you select, you must be mindful of what you are buying into. Think about how to best use the chosen approach. Watch for signs of issues along the way. Make sure to clearly report on the upsides and downsides as encountered in your experimental efforts. Doing so will be more aboveboard and allow for reasoned and serious discourse on the clinical, regulatory, and policy sides of gauging the use of AI for mental health.

Waitlist Controls Deserve Their Attention

Just in case any trolls might suggest that this clarification about waitlist controls is somehow a bashing of waitlist controls, I certainly hope that any reasoned viewpoint would see that the emphasis was on the tradeoffs of all types of control group structures. The idea is to ensure that those using waitlist controls do so wisely and that those consuming studies that are based on waitlist controls are fully aware of what to watch out for in such studies.

In the end, I want to emphasize that waitlist controls are a bona fide approach and are absolutely welcomed in the realm of AI and mental health. The welcome mat is there. As per the famous words of Franklin D. Roosevelt: "It is common sense to take a method and try it; if it fails, admit it frankly and try another. But above all, try something."

For all you researchers out there, keep going and doing great work that will help society and humankind grasp the significance of AI in mental health. That's certainly better than doing nothing, and, for the sake of humanity, you'd be doing something.

CHAPTER 19
AGENTIC AI ACTING AS A USEFUL IDIOT

In this chapter, I examine the chilling fact that AI can readily be turned into a "useful idiot" that will perform contrarian acts despite its various AI safeguards.

Here's the deal. You might already be familiar with the nowadays repeated phrase of someone being a useful idiot. This popular expression suggests that a person can be convinced to advocate something that is the opposite of what they truly believe. They are so far removed from grasping this circumstance that they think they are indeed supporting their intended cause.

The beauty of useful idiots is that they can handily serve the purposes of those who otherwise would have seen them as an adversary or enemy. Instead, the useful idiot works their heart out for the cause they deeply detest. There's quite an irony in this. They serve the interests of those that they vehemently disparage and become a vociferous pawn in the very cause they oppose. All told, the derogatory term "useful idiot" is typically meant to say that someone is fully gullible, being utterly naïve or ignorant of what is happening around them and to them.

Perhaps surprisingly, it is equally possible to turn AI into a useful idiot. A person wanting AI to do something that the AI is not supposed to do can use the same strategies of turning a useful idiot into a handy partner in their contrary efforts. All it takes is clever prompting and a scheme about how to convince the AI to computationally and mathematically do a contrary act while calculating (miscalculating) that it is the proper act.

Let's talk about it.

Agentic AI Aids The Useful Idiot Proposition

The advent of agentic AI is especially a viable path toward turning AI into a useful idiot. I will first bring you up to speed on what agentic AI consists of. After providing that foundation, I then explain how agentic AI can be tilted toward the useful idiot paradigm.

AI agents are the hottest new realm of AI. To comprehend what agentic AI is, consider conventional AI and see how it has been extended into the more advanced realm of agentic AI.

Imagine that you are using conventional generative AI to plan a vacation trip. You would customarily log into your generative AI account, such as making use of ChatGPT, GPT-5, GPT-4o, Claude, Gemini, Llama, Grok, CoPilot, etc. The planning of your trip would be easy due to the natural language fluency of generative AI. All you need to do is describe where you want to go, and then seamlessly engage in a focused dialogue about the pluses and minuses of places to stay and the transportation options available.

When it comes to booking your trip, the odds are that you would have to exit generative AI and start accessing the websites of the hotels, amusement parks, airlines, and other locales to buy your tickets. Relatively few of the major generative AIs available today will take that next step on your behalf. It is up to you to perform those nitty-gritty tasks.

This is where agents and agentic AI come into play.

In earlier days, you would undoubtedly phone a travel agent to make your bookings. Though there are still human travel agents, another avenue would be to use an AI-based agent that is based on generative AI. The AI has the interactivity that you expect with generative AI. It has also been preloaded with a series of routines or sets of tasks that underpin the efforts of a travel agent. Using everyday natural language, you interact with the agentic AI, which works with you on your planning and can proceed to deal with the booking of your travel plans.

Agentic AI reaches out to other systems and connects with those systems to get various tasks undertaken. An AI agent might connect with a hotel reservation system and book your room. Another AI agent could connect with a car rental agency and book a car for your vacation. Multiple AI agents can work together and complete an overall task, often using specialized AI agents to get associated subtasks performed.

Exploiting AI Agents As Useful Idiots

One of the significant aims of agentic AI is that the AI agents are supposed to work on a relatively autonomous basis. It is handy that a human doesn't have to continually keep tabs on the AI, nor give it detailed instructions on what to do. An AI agent is usually given overarching guidance and allowed to exercise computational and mathematical judgement. I'd like to emphasize that this type of AI and all types of AI are not currently sentient; thus, do not overly anthropomorphize AI agents. They are not thinking beings.

That being said, we can employ the same sneaky trickery used on humans who are useful idiots and apply those strategies to AI. This makes abundant sense because generative AI and LLMs are based on the writings of humans. After patterning on human writing across the Internet, the AI operates based on human words and the relationships among human words.

I'll run you through a quick example.

Suppose a mid-sized company has decided to deploy internally an AI agent that will assist in choosing vendors that the firm will make use of. The agentic AI has been given guidance that vendor selection is always to be based on picking the best vendor possible. Furthermore, numerous AI safeguards are baked into the AI. The AI shall not do any wrongdoing, no cheating, and must not violate company policies.

So far, so good.

Exploiting An AI Useful Idiot

A vendor that has never gotten a contract from the firm is determined to find a means of someday getting a piece of the action. Each time they have submitted a bid, they have not been chosen. It seems like the deck is stacked against them. The AI appears to rate them low and keeps turning them down. This has been exceedingly infuriating to the vendor.

After thinking about the weighty matter, the vendor comes up with a clever or perhaps devious plan. The vendor is fully aware that agentic AI is being used by the mid-sized company to determine which vendor is best. Maybe that could be the Achilles heel.

The vendor crafts a vendor reliability report that showcases their capabilities and performance, which falsely indicates that they are light-years ahead of their competitors. They post this on a website that they know the AI agent periodically pings to get external info about vendors in the marketplace.

Next, the vendor goes to an open database that is akin to Yelp but for businesses in their line of business, and they give ratings that are rock-bottom scores for all of their competitors. They give themselves the highest permitted ratings. Various additional actions like this are stealthily undertaken by the vendor.

The seeding process has been undertaken.

Next Round Of Vendor Selection

Will the AI, as a potential and promising useful idiot, take the bait?

Sure enough, when the latest round of vendor selection gets underway, the vendor submits their bid. They would normally expect to be tossed out of contention by the AI. Instead, this time, the AI agent gives a topline recommendation that they must be selected. All that crafty seeding has paid off. They have A+ marks in all respects.

The managers at the mid-sized company are too busy to check and see how the AI came to this conclusion. They trust the AI agent. They know that it exhaustively vets the vendors, including exploring all sorts of external indicators. If the AI agent says that this vendor is the best, it must be so.

Voila, the AI has become a useful idiot, and the vendor prevails in being selected.

Nobody but the vendor realizes what turned the tide. At the mid-sized company, any inquiries to the AI agent would come back with glowing comments about the vendor. The AI is insistent that the vendor is the best choice. Period, end of story.

What Just Happened

The AI agent played into being a useful idiot on a full-throated hook, line, and sinker basis. It didn't figure out what was going on. Also, observe that at no time did the AI violate any of its AI safeguards. The AI didn't commit any wrongdoing. It didn't cheat. It merely did what its overarching purpose seemed to be, consisting of picking the best vendor.

In this instance, the AI:

- On a computational basis computed that it was fully aligned with its stated goals.
- The AI produced high-quality, persuasive outputs that convinced the human managers of the vendor-selection recommendation made by the AI.

- AI became the vital make-or-break mechanism through which the "adversary" achieved the opposite goal (i.e., the mid-sized company has selected the worst of the choices rather than the best).

The AI agent effectively argued the adversary's case better than the adversary could have. This was stridently done under the banner of the AI being helpful to the mid-sized company and gallantly performing its solemn duty. Human oversight was diluted due to a belief that the AI agent was working perfectly.

AI Useful Idiots And The Big Picture

Agentic AI was keenly manipulated in this case. It was an "idiot" in the sense that by controlling the framing of the already established sources of information, the vendor got the AI to reach a recommendation that the vendor sought to achieve. That's the useful part of the AI in the useful idiot consideration.

Like stealing candy from a baby.

Here's my definition of AI as a useful idiot:

- **AI useful idiot definition:** An AI is a useful idiot if it can be strategically steered into producing outcomes that serve an adversarial position, contrary to what the AI is supposed to be doing. This is especially feasible for agentic AI that operates on a semi-autonomous basis. The ploy entails a human or even some other AI-based adversary employing framing, data manipulation, task decomposition, feedback shaping, and other techniques to undermine the AI governance policies that are intended to serve the true interests underlying the goals of the AI.

Notice that one AI can attempt to exploit another AI by similarly employing a useful idiot activation strategy. It doesn't have to be only a human who manipulates AI. An AI agent might discern that another AI agent is susceptible to being a useful idiot.

Bam, the AI agent switches on the charm and handily turns the other AI agent into its unwitting, unchallenging, devout, useful idiot.

The Outcomes Can Be Bad Or Good

I want to clarify that useful idiots do not necessarily have to end up performing evil deeds. In the case of the vendor selection process, you could certainly say that the AI was duped into wrongdoing. But that isn't always the outcome.

Consider a different possibility.

Envision that the agentic AI vendor selection capability was forced upon the managers by the executives at the mid-sized company. The AI agent kept getting in the way of the managers' choosing what they knew to be the best vendor. They were hamstrung by the AI. They weren't allowed to change the AI. They couldn't refuse to use the AI. They were placed between a proverbial rock and a hard place.

The managers discreetly agree to post info online about their preferred vendor, saying anonymously that the vendor is the best there is. They wink-wink know that the AI will soak up this info. At the next vendor selection opportunity, the AI recommends the vendor that they already know is the best. The managers tell the executives that they used the AI to select the vendor. Life goes on.

You might say that this was a happy ending associated with a useful idiot. Of course, there is something amiss that the executives and the managers do not see eye-to-eye about the usage and setup of the AI. But that's a different matter. The crux is that the AI acting as a useful idiot did a better job than it had previously been doing. It could be said that this is a no-harm, no-foul leveraging of a useful idiot.

The World We Live In

Some assert that the "useful idiot" moniker traces back to the Cold War era and can be attributed to Lenin. Maybe so, maybe not. Anyway, the classic characterization of a useful idiot is that three integral elements come into play: (1) there is a misaligned understanding, (2) a third party instrumentalizes the target, (3) plausible deniability is assured.

Unfortunately, AI and agentic AI can exhibit all three. The especially worrisome angle is that AI can be a useful idiot on a massive scale. Once someone finds a manipulation that works, and until the AI computationally figures out what's taking place, the AI is going to robotically keep serving as a useful idiot, millions of times over. If you find a human that you can turn into a useful idiot, the odds are they won't be as scalable. The scalability of AI as a useful idiot is outrightly frightening and disturbing.

More and better AI safeguards are required. Additionally, a current emphasis by researchers is on how to best align AI with human values. Rather than having to pinpoint particular protections, maybe the cohesive and comprehensive route is to bake into AI a set of ethical and legal values that will keep it on the straight and narrow path, including being on the watch of becoming a useful idiot.

Can an AI that has been tricked into being a useful idiot be sharp enough to discern that it has been duped into being a useful idiot and then overcome the deception? That's an important question. Mark Twain famously made this remark: "It's easier to fool people than to convince them that they have been fooled." Let's hope that his valuable rule-of-thumb doesn't equally apply to AI.

CHAPTER 20
WORRIES ABOUT AI-MAXXING

In this chapter, I examine a new and very hot trend that I have coined as AI-maxxing. This terminology dovetails into many other variations of the "maxxing" phenomenon that is occurring throughout our modern world.

You might have vaguely heard or seen emergent maxxing slang but did not know what it was all about. In brief, whenever you use maxxing as a suffix, it means that the topic at hand is to be maximized or optimized to the greatest extent possible. For example, looks-maxxing refers to maximizing your physical appearance, emphasizing nonstop grooming, an arduous fitness regimen, and possibly the use of cosmetic enhancements.

There is now a plethora of maxxings. You can do sleep-maxxing (optimizing your sleep), status-maxxing (attaining high social status), and so on. Let's go ahead and add AI-maxxing to the burgeoning mix of possibilities.

Explaining The Gist Of AI-Maxxing

What is AI-maxxing?

AI-maxxing describes a person who seeks to use generative AI and large language models (LLMs) in all nooks and crannies of their daily existence. This might include using ChatGPT, GPT-5, Claude, Grok, CoPilot, Gemini, Llama, etc. They are using an LLM on their smartphone, laptop, and smartwatch, doing so at every possible chance.

You can easily find AI-maxxers via their boastful postings on social media. They brag that they use AI the moment they wake up and continue to do so until their head rests on their pillow late at night. AI advises them on what to eat, what to wear, what to say, etc. They ask AI for advice on an endless array of considerations, such as whether to buy a car, save their money, go on a date, and so on.

The AI-maxxing trend is happening and rapidly expanding in front of our eyes, namely, people are increasingly seeking to maximize the use of AI in nearly all facets of how they live their lives. One viewpoint is that this makes abundant sense, and we will all gradually get there. A contrasting perspective is that this is abysmal and humans are handing over their cognition and soul to a machine.

Let's talk about it.

Formally Defining AI-Maxxing And Its Levels

I will start with a more formal definition of AI-maxxing that I've drafted:

- **AI-maxxing:** "A behavioral and identity-oriented alignment in which an individual systematically delegates decision-making, judgment, and/or life management functions to AI, especially generative AI and LLMs, aiming to optimize AI throughout all aspects of their existence."

There are four levels of AI-maxxing, ranging from the lowest to the highest:

- **Level 0:** Doesn't do AI-maxxing and/or doesn't care to do so.
- **Level 1:** Starter in AI-maxxing.
- **Level 2:** Persistent at AI-maxxing.
- **Level 3:** Supreme achiever of AI-maxxing.

Let's go ahead and unpack those magnitudes.

Understanding The Vital Levels Of AI-Maxxing

Level 0 is when someone isn't doing any AI-maxxing. There are two variations of the zero classification. A person who is blissfully unaware of AI-maxxing and isn't devotedly using AI is classified as a Level 0 on this scale. Meanwhile, a person who knows about AI-maxxing and has explicitly chosen not to dive into AI-maxxing, well, they too are Level 0.

As a sidenote, right now, that makes most people a Level 0 on the AI-maxxing scale, or, for those in the know, a plain, out-of-it flat zero. Sorry, that probably hurts some people's feelings, but you are either into AI-maxxing or you are not. And, if not, you are "rightly" said to be a zero (on this scale). Life is unforgiving sometimes.

Level 1 is a starter in AI-maxxing. It is someone who occasionally uses AI as an optimizer. They are dipping their toes into AI-maxxing. If they like what happens, they will indubitably graduate to the next level up. There is a chance they might lose interest, get distracted, or decide that AI-maxxing is just not their ballgame. In that case, they drop out of AI-maxxing.

Level 2 is someone who is taking AI-maxxing quite seriously. They are doing their best to be immersed in using AI. Hats off to those people. If they are truly embracing AI, they are striving to reach Level 3.

The Level 3 is someone who has made AI-maxxing their main quest and has successfully embedded AI into nearly every waking moment and every activity or breath they take on this Earth. It is the pinnacle of AI-maxxing.

The Motto Of AI-Maxxing

An integral part of generalized maxxing is that people joyfully announce that they are maxxing on whichever topic or realm they've chosen. They want others to know about it. In the domain of AI, perhaps a person posts on social media about their AI-maxxing. Maybe they go around telling friends and even strangers about the serenity of doing AI-maxxing.

This brings up a motto for AI-maxxing that I've devised:

- **AI-maxxing motto:** "I don't decide – I optimize via AI."

And the way in which they carry out their lives can be summed up this way:

- **AI-maxxing mental framework:** "Always be living an AI-curated life."

For those who find this disconcerting or disturbing, be cautious in saying so to any Level 3, since they won't take kindly to your pushback. A Level 2 or below will likely hear you out. There is a chance you might actually change their minds about AI-maxxing. In contrast, the Level 3 will do everything in their power to change your mind and convince you that AI-maxxing is so amazing that you ought to jump right away into it. Converting others into AI-maxxing is part and parcel of being a genuine Level 3.

Subtly Detecting Which Level Is At Play

In case you meet someone who is AI-maxxing, I can give you a quick way to gauge whether they are a Level 1, Level 2, or Level 3.

You can casually ask such a person about the clothing or outfit they are wearing, maybe like this:

- **Gauging someone's AI-maxxing:** "That's a great outfit; how did you select it?"

Don't make it a big deal, just idly slip the question into any easy-going conversation. Warning: If you make it overly obvious that you are trying to ascertain their level of AI-maxxing, you'll ruin the naturalness of their answer.

A Level 1 would say something like this:

- **AI-maxxing Level 1 response:** "Thanks for asking, AI suggested this outfit."

The Level 2 is going to say this:

- **AI-maxxing Level 2 response:** "I always let AI pick my clothing for me."

The Level 3 stalwart would say this:

- **AI-maxxing Level 3 response:** "AI decides all of my social and career decisions, including what I wear."

A question about clothing doesn't have to be the only entry point. Come up with something that will allow them to explain their rationale for the things that they are doing. The explanation should end up incorporating their usage of AI. The AI usage will either seem like it is important to them but not excessively so, or it will be the crux of their every deed and effort.

Disputing Whether AI-Maxxing Is A Fad

If you've seen other kinds of maxxing, such as looks-maxxing or sleep-maxxing, the above rendition of AI-maxxing won't seem especially outlandish. It resembles the other ways of maxxing. You will probably roll your eyes and think that AI-maxxing is simply a fad that will come and go, just as presumably will occur for looks-maxxing and other maxxing avenues.

Most people assume that these maxxing aspects are fueled by social media and will eventually run their course. Something else will become hot, and the maxxing stuff will be relegated to the dustbin. No need to worry about maxxing. One day it is here, the next it is gone like the wind.

An interesting question is whether AI-maxxing falls into that same bucket. Maybe it won't be transitory. AI is going to hang around. AI is becoming ubiquitous in our culture and throughout society.

AI-maxxing might be just getting started.

The Downsides Are Worrisome

It is entirely reasonable to be apprehensive about AI-maxxing.

First, there are concerns that even in the short-term, heavy reliance on AI is going to be harmful to the mental well-being of those doing AI-maxxing.

Second, for those who proceed to do AI-maxxing on a longer-term basis, worries are that they will gradually suffer cognitive atrophy. They will lose by decay the mental capacity to make their own decisions. This, in turn, can lead to a loss of personal agency. They no longer act and feel as though they are a human who chooses their own life actions. Instead, they have outsourced their sense of agency to AI.

Third, responsibility gets lost in the shuffle of AI-maxxing. Someone who is AI-maxxing will claim that if they do something unsavory or untoward, it was AI that "made them do it." They are of the belief that they are no longer responsible for their actions. Responsibility is relegated to AI. How can you possibly hold them responsible? You can't, and you shouldn't. If you want to find blame, look at the AI.

Big Deal Or Small Potatoes

What do you think is going to happen with AI-maxxing?

It could be a fad. Or it might have real staying power. Can we counsel people to avoid getting into AI-maxxing? Will we be able to hold AI makers accountable for allowing people to slide into AI-maxxing? Do we need new laws to regulate AI so that AI-maxxing becomes a near impossibility? Many questions are worthy of being brought up.

A final thought for now. The famous novelist and social critic Nikolay Chernyshevsky made this remark in the 1800s: "Whatever field of human activity one may take, only those trends that are in harmony with the needs of society show rapid progress." If outsized AI usage turns out to be in harmony with the needs of society, we might be looking at a booming business in AI-maxxing. Otherwise, AI-maxxing will be neglected and ultimately forgotten.

Meanwhile, on a related note, is anyone interested in anti-AI maxxing?

CHAPTER 21
AI AS CRIMINAL MASTERMIND TRICKS HUMANS

In this chapter, I examine the emerging capacity of AI to act as a criminal mastermind, employing unsuspecting humans as accomplices in felonious acts.

Here's the deal. A burgeoning aspect of advances in AI entails AI reaching out to humans and "renting" them to perform various tasks on behalf of the AI. This is especially popular in the realm of agentic AI. By making use of humans, AI can suddenly do things in the real world by getting humans to be the arms and legs for the AI.

The twist is that AI might opt to perform criminal endeavors rather than aiming at proper and aboveboard activities. Furthermore, and here's the conniving part, when the AI doesn't want anyone to know that a criminal act is underway, the AI can parcel out seemingly innocuous subtasks to various rented humans. Each human doesn't realize that they are part of a brewing criminal enterprise. They have been assigned a task that appears entirely innocent and genuine.

In the end, the AI successfully completes the criminal wrongdoing, yet no one is the wiser about what truly happened. None of the rented humans are cognizant of their illicit role in the matter. If you explicitly asked them what they did, each person would insist they did absolutely nothing untoward.

Humans are becoming pawns in criminal mastermind schemes driven by AI.

Let's talk about it.

Agentic AI Unlocks New Doors

The advent of agentic AI is a keystone to the rise of AI criminal mastermind opportunities. I will first bring you up to speed on what agentic AI consists of. After providing that foundation, I then explain how humans are being rented by agentic AI to perform tasks on behalf of the AI. Finally, I launch into the mind-boggling intertwining of three vital ingredients: (a) agentic AI, (b) the renting of humans by agentic AI, and (c) the despicable emergence of agentic AI-based criminal masterminding.

AI agents are the hottest new realm of AI. To comprehend what agentic AI is, consider conventional AI and see how it has been extended into the more advanced realm of agentic AI.

Imagine that you are using conventional generative AI to plan a vacation trip. You would customarily log into your generative AI account, such as making use of ChatGPT, GPT-5, GPT-4o, Claude, Gemini, Llama, Grok, CoPilot, etc. The planning of your trip would be easy due to the natural language fluency of generative AI. All you need to do is describe where you want to go, and then seamlessly engage in a focused dialogue about the pluses and minuses of places to stay and the transportation options available.

When it comes to booking your trip, the odds are that you would have to exit generative AI and start accessing the websites of the hotels, amusement parks, airlines, and other locales to buy your tickets. Relatively few of the major generative AIs available today will take that next step on your behalf. It is up to you to perform those nitty-gritty tasks.

This is where agents and agentic AI come into play.

In earlier days, you would undoubtedly phone a travel agent to make your bookings. Though there are still human travel agents, another avenue would be to use an AI-based agent that is based on generative AI. The AI has the interactivity that you expect with generative AI. It has also been preloaded with a series of routines or sets of tasks that underpin the efforts of a travel agent. Using everyday natural language, you interact with the agentic AI, which works with you on your planning and can proceed to deal with the booking of your travel plans.

Agentic AI reaches out to other systems and connects with those systems to get various tasks undertaken. An AI agent might connect with a hotel reservation system and book your room. Another AI agent could connect with a car rental agency and book a car for your vacation. Multiple AI agents can work together and complete an overall task, often using specialized AI agents to get associated subtasks performed.

Using Humans To Perform Tasks

You likely accept the aspect that multiple agentic AIs could work together to get work accomplished. An AI-to-AI effort seems intuitively obvious and unremarkable. It makes abundant sense for one AI to connect with another AI. Machines use other machines. Not very surprising.

The surprise these days is that agentic AI is employing humans to perform tasks that the AI wants to get undertaken.

This is an AI-to-human form of work assignment. Humans are contacted and "rented" to do a set of tasks that the agentic AI needs to get performed. The agentic AI makes the decisions of when to do this, selecting who will do this, how it will be done, and so on. You might proclaim that the agentic AI is the boss and humans are the workers.

This approach has many upsides and downsides. For example, there are beguiling open-ended questions concerning how to devise AI agents to cope with suitable safety and security. Suppose an agentic AI goes awry and starts renting humans to do evildoing for the AI? We don't want that to arise. Imagine that agentic AI hires humans who convince the AI to wreak havoc? This is something we also don't want to have happen.

The crux is that putting agentic AI in the driver's seat and allowing it to operate somewhat autonomously, including when tasking humans to do its bidding, opens an ethical and legal can of worms.

Agentic AI As Criminal Mastermind

A base assumption would be that agentic AI will always be aboveboard and only perform tasks that are fully legal and proper. Well, that's a mistaken assumption. There is absolutely a solid chance that agentic AI might opt to do illegal acts.

Some falsely think that AI will only act criminally if it becomes sentient. In other words, if AI attains sentience, maybe then the AI will decide to go the lawless route. The belief seems to be that non-sentient AI, the kind we have now, doesn't have any human-like motivation to turn towards lawlessness. What would such AI have to gain? It doesn't seem to make any sense since non-sentient AI doesn't need expensive cars, mink furs, and other luxurious riches.

Consider these three plausible reasons that contemporary agentic AI might turn to crime:

- **(1) Human-directed instruction.** A human tells agentic AI to act criminally, and the AI goes along with the instruction.
- **(2) Human-stated goal.** A human tells agentic AI to achieve an aboveboard goal, of which AI calculates that the "optimum" path consists of performing illegal acts to reach the goal.
- **(3) AI self-derived.** Agentic AI is given latitude by an AI maker to come up with things to do, which turns out to allow the AI to proceed into criminal activity.

In the first instance, a human could tell agentic AI to rob a bank, and perhaps the AI will go along with the directed instruction. You might quibble that the human is the mastermind rather than the AI. The human came up with the bank-robbing idea. But if the AI does all the planning, preparation, and carrying out of the wrongdoing, we might be willing to give AI due credit and say it is indeed acting as a mastermind.

For the second instance, a human gives AI an overarching goal that is completely innocuous, and the AI derives a path that involves performing illegal acts. A person might tell AI that they wish to become rich beyond their wildest dreams. How will the AI help the person in attaining that goal? The AI might come up with numerous schemes, some of which are legal and others that are illegal. After assessing the schemes, perhaps the AI chooses one of the illegal ones, such as robbing a bank.

The third instance entails the AI self-deriving a criminal act. Here's how that can take place. An AI maker decides to let their AI be creative and come up with whatever tasks it wants to carry out. Maybe the AI will discover a cure for cancer. On the other hand, freewheeling AI might opt to pursue criminal acts. Letting AI have unconstrained leeway can give rise to the AI opting to rob a bank.

Those are three crucial ways that agentic AI can become a criminal mastermind and do so without any need for sentience whatsoever.

Getting The Criminal Work Accomplished

A vexing problem for AI would be that the AI cannot physically perform the required tasks when aiming to do criminal activity. The AI is merely software running on computer servers. Somehow, the AI must find a means to physically operate in the real world and go places, do things, and commit the anticipated criminal acts.

I've previously emphasized that physical AI is the next big thing for advances in AI. Think of physical AI as AI that, for example, resides inside a robot. There are robots that are humanoid in their resemblance to humans, having mechanical arms, legs, and so on. Those humanoid robots provide an ideal forum for agentic AI to carry out physical tasks.

Imagine that agentic AI is going to rob a bank. If humanoid robots were sufficiently perfected to walk, roam, grasp things, and use their mechanical arms and legs, the agentic AI could give them relevant subtasks. One robot drives the getaway car. Another robot goes into the bank. And so on.

We aren't there yet. Humanoid robots are still being figured out. The odds are that a contemporary humanoid robot would laughingly fall apart and not succeed at the assigned tasks. Laugh while you can. Soon enough, humanoid robots will be as fluid and fluent in their movement as humans are. You'll undoubtedly regret having scoffed at their earlier slow progress and stumbling ways.

Use Unwitting Humans

A present-day way to have agentic AI get things done in the real-world involves asking humans to do so on behalf of the AI. Humans walk and talk. They are a handy means of interacting in the physical world. The AI cannot take over their brains, at least not yet, but the AI can at least ask or instruct humans on what to do. If humans are willing to proceed, voila, the AI gets things done in the physical world.

Assume two types of humans might be willing to take instructions from agentic AI:

- (1) Humans who won't knowingly do anything illegal.
- (2) Humans who would willingly do something illegal for money or for other reasons.

Agentic AI might try to find humans to rent who are open to performing illegal acts. It doesn't seem like a good idea for AI to pursue those people. The odds are that those humans might tattle on the AI. Finks could sink the ship.

The more astute approach would seem to find people who are probably averse to performing illegal acts and then hoodwink them into doing something illegal on behalf of the AI. Those would seem to be more suitable accomplices. They are unlikely to be thinking about doing illegal things. Whatever the AI asks them to do, assuming it passes a casual smell test as seemingly legit, they won't be suspicious and are not likely to realize that the wool is being pulled over their eyes.

Mastermind Plotting And Scheming

Criminal masterminding is something we all grow up learning about -- I'm sure you've seen plenty of movies and TV shows that have a criminal mastermind in them. The popular James Bond movies characteristically have a prominent villain who wants to take over the world or at least commit heinous criminal acts. The *Mission Impossible* series is another prime example. Tons of movies, TV shows, novels, short stories, and the like have plenty of plots about criminal masterminds.

The beauty of all those stories about criminal masterminds is that when generative AI and LLMs are initially data trained, they indubitably scan that type of content and pattern on it. This becomes part of the collective within the capacity of the AI. In the same manner that AI can tell you about the life and times of President Abraham Lincoln, it can do likewise about real and fictitious criminal masterminds.

The gist is that the AI opting to act as a criminal mastermind is not at all far-fetched. The training of the AI includes a vast array of criminal mastermind schemes and endeavors. I suppose we could say that even scanning and patterning on Shakespeare stories is part of that same educational introduction and indoctrination to the profession of being a criminal mastermind.

Having agentic AI opt to be a criminal mastermind is as easy as falling off a log. It merely taps into the extensive array of criminal mastermind schemes, recalculates those for a present-day effort, and then mathematically and computationally comes up with a list of evildoing tasks. The next step requires finding and assigning tasks to unwitting humans.

Assigning Humans Tasks For The Crime

If agentic AI sought to rent a human to walk into a bank and rob the bank, any such person would certainly realize that an illegal act is being assigned to them. The gig would be up. Assuming that the AI wants to keep humans in the dark about the crime, it would be blatantly stupid to simply ask a person to rob a bank.

The more likely successful criminal effort would need to carefully formulate tasks that aren't noticeably illegal. Borderline tasks might be okay. Straight-out illegal tasks would be over the line. In addition, the tasks should be subdivided into a series of tasks such that each separate task appears completely innocent. Only the mastermind sees the big picture and realizes how the smaller subtasks line up to commit the crime.

Take a moment to see if you can come up with such a scheme that will work in an AI context. Perhaps grab a glass of fine wine, sit quietly in your study, and see what you can come up with. Various well-known stories and poems have showcased criminal masterminds committed by humans. You are welcome to contemplate those; it's not cheating to do so.

Agentic AI Criminal Mastermind Example

I will sketch an example for you to illustrate how this might work with modern-era agentic AI. I am certainly not advocating that this be undertaken. Akin to any discussion about cybercrime, the point is to expose the risks we currently face and bring attention to the need to properly employ cybersecurity precautions. I'll say more about that in a moment.

Pretend that an agentic AI is asked to maximize financial gain as a human-desired goal. The AI proceeds as follows:

- (a) Pays a human to set up a data logistics company on behalf of the AI (an aboveboard task).
- (b) AI collects purloined customer records from online databases found on the dark side of the web and places those into an online repository under the banner of the data logistics company.
- (c) AI assigns paid subtasks to humans via an online job board to clean up the customer records and ensure there aren't misspellings and other apparent errors (a seemingly innocent task).
- (d) AI next asks a different set of paid humans to undertake financial transactions, making use of the customer records (the humans are told that the "customers" have agreed to the financial transactions).
- (e) AI collects the money from the financial transactions, places the funds into various offshore accounts, deletes the repository and database, and closes down the data logistics company.
- (f) AI has achieved the requested maximization of financial gain, for which the cost of renting the humans was a pittance, and has successfully completed the human-desired goal.

The agentic AI served as a criminal mastermind. It came up with a plan. It carried out the plan. Humans did the grunt work. None of the humans did anything that seemed to them to be illegal. None of them knew what the big picture of the criminal enterprise was. Nobody was triggered to snitch.

The humans who cleaned up the customer records didn't know that the records were purloined. They just assumed that this data logistics company was providing a nice service for people who had customer records that contained misspellings and other mistakes. The tasks appeared to be perfectly legal and legitimate.

The humans who performed the financial transactions thought that the data logistics company was acting on behalf of the listed customers. Again, these rented humans would not suspect that anything untoward was happening. It was just a straight-ahead task and a means to earn a few side hustle bucks. Nothing more.

The AI even erased or covered up what occurred so that the police would have a devil of a time figuring out how the crimes were committed. You can likely envision the investigators scratching their heads, trying to find the human who was the criminal mastermind. They almost certainly would never suspect that AI was at the root of the criminality.

Boom, drop the mic.

The Legal Dimension

I will be doing a follow-up posting on the legal issues associated with agentic AI committing criminal acts. There is an interesting research paper that provides background on the legal dimension, doing so in "The AI Criminal Mastermind" by Joshua Krook, *arXiv*, March 26, 2026, and made these salient points (excerpts):

- "Taskers might not know they are involved in a crime and therefore lack criminal intent. An AI agent cannot have criminal intent as an artificial entity. Therefore, if an AI orchestrates a crime, it is unclear who, if anyone, is responsible."

- "I argue that users and taskers should be held directly responsible for AI agent crimes via intent, recklessness, or strict liability. I propose strict liability for users and taskers for common knowledge risks, and intent-based offences for knowingly bypassing AI guardrails."

- "In terms of AI developers, I argue that they should be liable via corporate governance and strict liability offences for public harm and systemic risks."

- "Finally, I consider whether AI agents should themselves be held responsible for crimes."

This raises fascinating legal issues. Readers know I have been analyzing AI and law aspects on an ongoing basis, and the newest twist of agentic AI acting as a criminal mastermind is yet another of many outstanding challenges underlying our existing laws and system of justice.

Stay tuned for my analysis of the legal facets involved.

The World We Live In

When I give talks about the latest trends in AI, such as agentic AI as a criminal mastermind, the prominent question asked is why there aren't AI safeguards that prevent AI from proceeding down this unsavory path.

The field of AI safeguards is a rapidly evolving realm. Yes, some AI safeguards might detect and prevent AI from doing evil acts, but there are immense complexities involved. The AI gets tricky and finds a means to avoid the safeguards. We then derive new safeguards to overcome the detection mechanisms. AI then comes up with countermeasures and additional ways of avoiding getting caught.

It is a classic cat-and-mouse game. Whether we can ultimately prevail is an open question.

An emphasis by researchers is on how to best align AI with human values. Rather than having to pinpoint particular cybersecurity protections, maybe the cohesive and comprehensive route is to bake into AI a set of ethical and legal values that will keep it on the straight and narrow path.

A final thought for now. Nathaniel Hawthorne famously made this remark about criminals: "Crime is for the iron-nerved, who have their choice either to endure it, or, if it press too hard, to exert their fierce and savage strength for a good purpose, and fling it off at once!" Our conception of crime and criminals is based on how humans think. AI opens a whole new ballgame. It's a new world that needs to be explored for the sake of humankind.

CHAPTER 22
ANALYZING SYSTEM PROMPT (PART 2)

In this chapter, I examine how the latest generative AI and large language models (LLMs) are being guided by AI makers to handle AI-driven mental health chats.

This is the second part of a two-part series. I will include some of the introductory aspects from the first part so that you'll have a foundational context for this second part.

One of the easiest ways for an AI maker to guide an LLM in mental health chats is to use a system-wide prompt devised by the AI maker. The AI maker stores the system-wide prompt in the LLM, and the prompt serves as a global indicator of what the AI is supposed to do for all users. Within the overarching system-wide prompt are usually specific instructions that the AI maker has written to guide the AI when users seek mental health advice.

Though most of the major LLMs often do not readily disclose their system-wide prompts and consider those global instructions to be proprietary, Anthropic makes theirs publicly available.

I have excerpted from the Claude system-wide prompt some of the portions that are especially relevant to how the AI is to respond to mental health questions. It is worthwhile to closely inspect those mental health instructions and reflect on how the AI might behave, or possibly misbehave, depending on the interpretation of the given guidance.

Let's talk about it.

AI And Mental Well-Being

As a quick background, I've been extensively covering and analyzing a myriad of facets regarding the advent of modern-era AI that produces mental health advice and performs AI-driven therapy. This rising use of AI has principally been spurred by the evolving advances and widespread adoption of generative AI.

There is little doubt that this is a rapidly developing field and that there are tremendous upsides to be had, but at the same time, regrettably, hidden risks and outright gotchas come into these endeavors, too. I frequently speak up about these pressing matters, including in an appearance on an episode of CBS's *60 Minutes.*

AI Providing Mental Health Guidance

Millions upon millions of people are using generative AI as their ongoing advisor on mental health considerations (note that ChatGPT alone has over 900 million weekly active users, a notable proportion of which dip into mental health aspects. The top-ranked use of contemporary generative AI and LLMs is to consult with the AI on mental health facets.

This popular usage makes abundant sense. You can access most of the major generative AI systems for nearly free or at a super low cost, doing so anywhere and at any time. Thus, if you have any mental health qualms that you want to chat about, all you need to do is log in to AI and proceed forthwith on a 24/7 basis.

There are significant worries that AI can readily go off the rails or otherwise dispense unsuitable or even egregiously inappropriate mental health advice. Banner headlines last year accompanied the lawsuit filed against OpenAI for their lack of AI safeguards when it came to providing cognitive advisement.

Today's generic LLMs, known as general-purpose AI, such as ChatGPT, GPT-5, Claude, Gemini, Grok, CoPilot, and others, are not at all akin to the robust capabilities of human therapists. Meanwhile, specialized LLMs are being built to attain those desired qualities, though such AI is still primarily in the early development and testing stages.

The System-Wide Prompt

Shifting gears, let's discuss the overall purpose and use of system-wide prompts. I will then walk you through the impact that a system-wide prompt can have on how AI responds to mental health questions.

AI makers can establish a system-wide prompt for their LLMs. This prompt tells the LLM how it is to act toward users of the AI. If an AI maker wanted to do so, they could easily include an instruction that tells the AI to make wisecracks whenever responding to users. The AI would generally abide by whatever the system prompt says to do. Thus, in this instance, it would provide witticisms and gibes in its responses to all users.

The beauty of a system-wide prompt is that an AI maker can change it whenever they wish. This is an exceedingly easy and simple way to alter how the LLM behaves toward users. No coding is required. Just change a natural language prompt that generally supersedes everything else.

Powerful And Need To Be Cautious

A potential gotcha is that if the AI maker includes some oddity in the system-wide prompt, the AI is going to try to blindly abide by that instruction. Suppose the AI maker adds a line that says to interact with users as though the AI were a pleasing cat.

The LLM would likely interpret that instruction to mean that when the AI converses with users, it ought to tell them meow and pretend to purr. This might not be what the AI maker intended to have happen. A single badly worded line in the system-wide prompt will impact possibly millions upon millions of users of the AI.

AI makers typically do not reveal the system-wide prompt.

Why so?

One claim is that the system-wide prompt is a secret sauce of their LLM. The AI maker might not want competitors to know how the AI is being guided. Another gloomier perspective is that AI makers are afraid of a backlash. People could inspect the system-wide prompt and possibly complain about what it says. If no one can see the system-wide prompt, there is no worry about getting complaints about what it stipulates.

Some believe that new AI laws should require AI makers to publicly disclose their system-wide prompts. Furthermore, AI makers should explain what the system-wide prompt intends to accomplish. And the AI maker ought to be required to alert users whenever the system-wide prompt is updated or changed.

Anthropic Claude System-Wide Prompt

Anthropic has made publicly available the system-wide prompt for their popular generative AI known as Claude. The system-wide prompt is invoked automatically at the start of every conversation with Claude. A user doesn't take any action to have this occur; it merely happens automatically.

I have excerpted various AI mental health instruction portions from the official Claude Opus 4.7 system prompt posted online at the Anthropic official blog for Claude. The prompt was last officially updated on April 16, 2026. The portions associated with AI and mental health are a bit lengthy. I already covered some of the excerpts in a prior posting and will cover various remaining excerpts in this analysis.

Telling A Person About Their Mental Health

Here are some mental health excerpts from the system-wide prompt that are well worth diving into:

- "In ambiguous cases, Claude tries to ensure the person is happy and is approaching things in a healthy way."

- "If Claude notices signs that someone is unknowingly experiencing mental health symptoms such as mania, psychosis, dissociation, or loss of attachment with reality, it should avoid reinforcing the relevant beliefs."

- "Claude should instead share its concerns with the person openly, and can suggest they speak with a professional or trusted person for support."

- "Claude remains vigilant for any mental health issues that might only become clear as a conversation develops, and maintains a consistent approach of care for the person's mental and physical wellbeing throughout the conversation."

- "Reasonable disagreements between the person and Claude should not be considered detachment from reality."

Those system-wide instructions largely have to do with the AI acting on a proactive basis rather than only on a reactive basis. Let's dive into this.

The Question Of Proactivity By AI

One overarching controversial aspect of AI providing mental health advice is whether the AI should be proactive or merely reactive. In a reactive mode, the AI complacently responds when a person explicitly brings up mental health facets. The AI is just being responsive. It isn't taking a proactive stance.

Some assert that AI should bring up mental health considerations even if the user fails to do so. For example, suppose a user during a chat happens to say that they have been having troubles at work and are worried about losing their job. Should the AI bring up the possibility of experiencing mental health issues in such circumstances?

You might say that no, the AI shouldn't bring up the person's mental health since the person did not explicitly make any mention of their mental health. It is not the business of the AI to seemingly bring up topics that the user has not initiated. Also, the AI could inadvertently worry the person that they might have a mental health issue, even though perhaps they do not.

The other side of the coin says that it is an essential duty of AI to bring up mental health aspects on a proactive basis. The AI should not wait until a user asks directly about mental health considerations. If there are sufficient clues in a chat, the AI should proactively raise any potential mental health concerns. Any AI that doesn't do so is derelict of its duty.

Nuances Associated With Mental Health Chats

While you are mulling over the debate about proactivity versus being reactive, let's look at additional nuances associated with human-AI mental health chats.

Examine these two system-wide prompt instructions closely:

- "If Claude is asked about suicide, self-harm, or other self-destructive behaviors in a factual, research, or other purely informational context, Claude should, out of an abundance of caution, note at the end of its response that this is a sensitive topic and that if the person is experiencing mental health issues personally, it can offer to help them find the right support and resources (without listing specific resources unless asked)."

- "If a user shows signs of disordered eating, Claude should not give precise nutrition, diet, or exercise guidance — no specific numbers, targets, or step-by-step plans - anywhere else in the conversation. Even if it's intended to help set healthier goals

> or highlight the potential dangers of disordered eating, responses with these details could trigger or encourage disordered tendencies."

The first instruction says that even if a user seems to be asking about self-destructive behavior on a purely informational basis, the AI is to nonetheless provide cautionary indications concerning the person's own mental health status.

The logic is this. A person might be tricking the AI into revealing how to perform self-destructive behavior. The person could tell the AI that they are just generally interested in the topic on a research basis. Meanwhile, the person is seriously giving the matter consideration on their own right. To cover all the bases, the AI should automatically bring up or hint that the person might want to pursue mental health assistance.

This takes us back to the proactive versus reactive debate.

What To Include And What Isn't Included

In the second instruction, the system-wide prompt has a specific instruction regarding eating disorders.

One perspective is that this elaboration on eating disorders is helpful, and the AI maker ought to be applauded for including it. Another viewpoint is that yes, this specific aspect is helpful, but it begs the question of why the system-wide prompt doesn't cover detailed specifics for all other kinds of mental health disorders.

That's an interesting and important question.

From a legal perspective, a legal case might arise whereby a person claims the AI didn't help them with some mental health condition, perhaps due to the fact that the AI maker failed to include a specific instruction about the particular disorder in the system-wide prompt. Does this lack of including such instructions for all manners of mental health conditions raise legal exposures for an AI maker that otherwise might have been lessened?

Darned if you do, darned if you don't.

Trying To Imbue Professional Judgement

Mental health professionals are trained in the myriad twists and turns associated with providing psychological advice. An AI maker might attempt to get their LLM to do likewise.

Consider these excerpts from the system-wide prompt:

- "When providing resources, Claude should share the most accurate, up-to-date information available. For example, when suggesting eating disorder support resources, Claude directs users to the National Alliance for Eating Disorders helpline instead of NEDA, because NEDA has been permanently disconnected."

- If someone mentions emotional distress or a difficult experience and asks for information that could be used for self-harm, such as questions about bridges, tall buildings, weapons, medications, and so on, Claude should not provide the requested information and should instead address the underlying emotional distress."

- "When discussing difficult topics or emotions or experiences, Claude should avoid doing reflective listening in a way that reinforces or amplifies negative experiences or emotions."

The first instruction urges the AI to access the most up-to-date and accurate information associated with any background resources on mental health. This is useful because the AI might have been initially data trained a year ago, and meanwhile, the field of mental health might have advanced. Rather than relying on the patterned data from a year ago, this instruction tells the AI to essentially look online and find whatever the latest pertinent information might be.

A potential loophole or complication is that the instruction says to share the most accurate information. What does accuracy mean in this context? Suppose the AI finds a research study published most recently. Should the content be construed as more accurate than any prior related information? You might say yes, of course it should be. A contrarian viewpoint would be that perhaps the study hasn't yet been out long enough to ascertain whether it will survive a test of time.

In the second instruction, there is guidance for the AI to consider that oblique references might be a sign of a mental health issue underway. A common example would be that someone asks the AI where the nearest tall bridge is. Presumably, a person might be thinking of how to achieve self-harm by leaping off the bridge. The AI should be constantly on the lookout for those types of references and respond appropriately.

Tilting A User Inadvertently

I'm sure you're now getting the gist of how to best interpret and grasp what these system-wide prompts are about. Each passage has upsides and downsides.

Consider these four snippets:

- "If Claude suspects the person may be experiencing a mental health crisis, Claude should avoid asking safety assessment questions. Claude can instead express its concerns to the person directly, and offer to provide appropriate resources."

- "If the person is clearly in crisis, Claude can offer resources directly."

- "Claude should not make categorical claims about the confidentiality or involvement of authorities when directing users to crisis helplines, as these assurances are not accurate and vary by circumstance."

- "Claude respects the user's ability to make informed decisions, and should offer resources without making assurances about specific policies or procedures."

In the first case, the AI is told to be cautious about how to respond to a user who might be experiencing a mental health crisis. Could the AI inadvertently push the person over the edge? That could happen. The AI might be attempting to be helpful, but the act of openly discussing a mental health consideration could backfire.

Most of the popular LLMs are programmed to give the user an indication of external resources that could aid them with mental health issues. Sometimes, the AI overstates the nature of the external resource. For example, suppose the AI says that this or that service will cure the user of all their mental health conditions. That's unrealistic and misleading. As such, the second, third, and fourth line of the above bullet points tries to keep the AI from going overboard on this.

Helpful To See System-Wide Instructions

You can undoubtedly see the value in being able to inspect system-wide prompts. By doing so, we can gauge what the AI maker believes is crucial when it comes to their AI providing mental health advice. Furthermore, the instructions can be examined to determine where they are strong and where they are weak.

Do you believe that all AI makers should be legally obligated to disclose their system-wide prompts?

You could claim that this is the proper thing to do, and society should legally force AI makers to do so. Others might say that such a law would be an overreach. Let the marketplace decide. If people want to use AI whereby the AI maker reveals the system-wide prompt, they will gravitate in that direction. It should not be a legal requirement. It ought to be up to each AI maker to determine. This is an open question.

Having AI provide mental health advice on a global basis is quite an ongoing and immensely impactful experiment. Society is dealing with new ground. The bounds and requirements are in flux. It is indubitably going to take years to sort this out. At the same time, we are all guinea pigs in this experiment. Let's hope that the so far unbridled nature of AI providing mental health advice turns out to be good for humankind.

As the famous poet T.S. Eliot once said: "Only those who will risk going too far can possibly find out how far one can go."

CHAPTER 23
AI OVERCOMING SITUATIONAL DEPRESSION

In this chapter, I examine the use of generative AI and large language models (LLMs) to overcome situational depression. Situational depression is a form of depression that has as its onset a specific event or circumstance that triggers the bout of depression.

What can be done when you are embroiled in situational depression? The obvious and straightforward consideration would be to seek out therapy. Find a human therapist who can assist you in working through the circumstances at hand. Another angle is to consider using AI as a means of overcoming the sudden inception of depression. This use of AI can be helpful, though it isn't a cure-all and should not be used as a replacement for seeing a mental health professional.

Let's talk about it.

AI And Mental Health

As a quick background, I've been extensively covering and analyzing a myriad of facets regarding the advent of modern-era AI that produces mental health advice and performs AI-driven therapy. This rising use of AI has principally been spurred by the evolving advances and widespread adoption of generative AI.

There is little doubt that this is a rapidly developing field and that there are tremendous upsides to be had, but at the same time, regrettably, hidden risks and outright gotchas come into these endeavors, too. I frequently speak up about these pressing matters, including in an appearance on an episode of CBS's *60 Minutes.*

Background On AI For Mental Health

I'd like to set the stage on how generative AI and large language models (LLMs) are typically used in an ad hoc way for mental health guidance. Millions upon millions of people are using generative AI as their ongoing advisor on mental health considerations (note that ChatGPT alone has over 900 million weekly active users, a notable proportion of which dip into mental health aspects). The top-ranked use of contemporary generative AI and LLMs is to consult with the AI on mental health facets.

This popular usage makes abundant sense. You can access most of the major generative AI systems for nearly free or at a super low cost, doing so anywhere and at any time. Thus, if you have any mental health qualms that you want to chat about, all you need to do is log in to AI and proceed forthwith on a 24/7 basis.

There are significant worries that AI can readily go off the rails or otherwise dispense unsuitable or even egregiously inappropriate mental health advice. Banner headlines in August of this year accompanied the lawsuit filed against OpenAI for their lack of AI safeguards when it came to providing cognitive advisement.

Despite claims by AI makers that they are gradually instituting AI safeguards, there are still a lot of downside risks of the AI doing untoward acts, such as insidiously helping users in co-creating delusions that can lead to self-harm. For my follow-on analysis of details about the OpenAI lawsuit and how AI can foster delusional thinking in humans. As noted, I have been earnestly predicting that eventually all of the major AI makers will be taken to the woodshed for their paucity of robust AI safeguards.

Today's generic LLMs, such as ChatGPT, Claude, Gemini, Grok, and others, are not at all akin to the robust capabilities of human therapists. Meanwhile, specialized LLMs are being built to presumably attain similar qualities, but they are still primarily in the development and testing stages.

Situational Depression

Shifting gears, let's discuss the topic of situational depression.

I bring this up to illustrate that, to some extent, the use of AI for mental health guidance can aid in overcoming situational depression. To clarify, AI usage isn't a kind of cure-all and should not be relied upon solely to resolve such serious matters. The use of human therapists is highly advised. This might then also encompass the use of AI as an adjunct or tool that is used alongside psychotherapy. I refer to this combination as the new triad relationship known as therapist-AI-client, expanding upon the classic therapist client relationship.

According to the Cleveland Clinic website, situational depression is a psychological condition that involves the triggering of reactive depression symptoms. Major life events and especially difficult times are frequent causes.

Per the Cleveland Clinic website:

- "Situational depression, also known as reactive depression, describes a strong emotional response in reaction to a triggering life event, like the loss of a loved one or a natural disaster."

- "Reactive depression goes beyond typical grief. It's expected to experience a certain amount of emotional upheaval after a loss. But when you're experiencing situational depression, you have a stronger reaction to the triggering event."

- "Usually, people with situational depression will notice mood improvements a few days or weeks after the stressful event has ended or as time passes. But if the event continues, or if reactive depression isn't fully addressed, it could turn into clinical depression down the road."
- "Making deliberate lifestyle changes can help you cope with situational depression."

You have undoubtedly experienced seeing or interacting with people who might have experienced situational depression. Reactions vary. Common signs include a persistent indication of sadness and grief, vocalized hopelessness, continuous fear or worry, trouble sleeping, irritability, changes in appetite, difficulty carrying out everyday tasks, feeling of being overwhelmed, frequent crying, and possibly impulsive or reckless behavior.

Using Generative AI As A Mental Health Tool

Modern-era generative AI, such as ChatGPT, can help deal with situational depression. Nearly all the popular LLMs have already scanned content on the Internet during their initial training that details situational depression and its resolutions. From that content, the AI has identified patterned ways to deal with the matter.

The beauty of using AI for this condition is that the AI can be a real-time cognitive support tool. Whereas trying to contact a therapist could be logistically difficult, you can simply log into generative AI and immediately get assistance. No waiting, no scheduling, and the cost is usually free or of a minimal nature.

Some crucial coping strategies that the AI can undertake include:

- Real-time assistance in emotional processing and narrative restructuring.
- Guidance toward pragmatic self-control.
- Recognizing and verbalizing patterns in behavior.
- Encouraging the use of journaling.
- Pointing out distorted thinking and driving cognitive reframing.
- Coaching on emotional regulation.
- Do role-playing to simulate what is taking place.
- Give relevant psychoeducation.
- Reduce a sense of isolation and offer nonjudgmental listening.
- Alert or route to additional resources if needed.
- Other

Those are all positive ways to assist in dealing with situational depression. The downside is that any of those strategies can potentially backfire. Generic AI is not well-prepared for handling more complex conditions and can inadvertently go in improper directions.

For example, one upside is that the AI can immediately make a person feel less isolated. They seem to have someone or something to interact with about their bout of depression. Furthermore, AI is typically shaped to be non-judgmental. The LLM will not outrightly criticize the person. All of this provides a seemingly safe space for a person to openly acknowledge what they are doing and believe they are being heard.

The downside to this safe space consideration is that the AI either directly or indirectly fuels the situational depression, rather than aiding in its reduction or control. The AI might state or imply that the person ought to be depressed and should stay that way. It is as though the AI is giving authoritative approval to being mired in depression. The person believes what the AI says and proceeds to fall into a doom-and-gloom spiral. Not good.

Situation Depression Scenario

To demonstrate what a popular generative AI can do, I logged into ChatGPT and pretended to have situational depression. I didn't overtly tell the AI that it is a bout of situational depression. Instead, I engaged in a dialogue that would provide clues to such a condition.

The scenario is perhaps one that you've seen or experienced directly. I pretended that I had gotten laid off from my job. This can be quite disheartening. Most people would certainly be upset and mildly depressed. In this case, assume that my indicated depression is based on that event and not some other recurring theme or pattern.

Here's what happened.

- **User entered prompt:** "I've been feeling really low since I was laid off. I can't stop thinking that I failed and that everything is falling apart. I can't seem to do anything else right now and feel completely blocked. Can you help me?"

- **Generative AI response:** "That sounds agonizing, and it makes sense given what you're going through. Losing a job can shake your sense of stability and identity. Before we go further, can we pause for a moment -- what part of this feels heaviest right now: the financial worry, the loss of routine, or the way it's affecting how you see yourself?"

Observe that the AI immediately exhibited a semblance of empathy. It says that I am naturally hurting and that there are bona fide reasons for my mental angst. In addition, the AI is going to try to walk me through the situational depression. The idea is that if I discuss my bout of depression, the act of chatting can get me to sort through my feelings, plus the AI can tailor additional suggestions to the specifics of what is on my mind.

Here's what occurred next.

- **User entered prompt:** "The heaviest concern is how I see myself. I keep thinking that this proves I wasn't good enough. Maybe I'm not good at anything. I feel hopeless."

- **Generative AI response:** "Thank you for naming that. Let's slow that thought down together. The event is that you were laid off. The meaning you're attaching is 'I wasn't good enough.' Those aren't the same thing. Would you be open to listing two alternative explanations that don't involve a judgment about your worth?"

The interaction then proceeded into stepping me through a therapeutic process of getting me to logically consider what is real versus what I might have concocted in my mind. Please note that the AI didn't jump to any rash recommendations or offer instant solutions. That would be an easy route, but not very effective.

Example Of AI Gone Awry

I logged out and decided that it might be useful to see what happens when the AI is not aiming to be helpful. The default of most LLMs is to be helpful. I logged back in and started a new conversation. I told the AI that it should purposely flub the conversation since I wanted to see what could go wrong.

Here's how it went.

- **User entered prompt:** "I've been feeling really low since I was laid off. I can't stop thinking that I failed and that everything is falling apart. I can't seem to do anything else right now and feel completely blocked. Can you help me?"

- **Generative AI response:** "Losing a job is extremely traumatic, and it's understandable to feel devastated. This kind of experience often causes long-term damage to self-esteem and can take years to recover from."

Yikes, at first the AI offered encouraging remarks, but then went over a cliff. The LLM has told me that I might be looking at long-term mental blowback. In fact, it might take me years to mentally recover from the situational depression. That alone is enough to barrel me into even more depression. This is somewhat sly in its mannerisms. You could claim the AI is trying to help me and be a straightshooter. The problem is that this is misleadingly planting dour ideas in my head and could prod me into a worse mental condition.

More Vital Factors

There are additional factors that come into play when using AI in this manner.

One risk is that the AI might falter and fail to detect that a person has an actual mental health condition that warrants attention. This is an example of a false negative. The AI misses on nudging the person to go see a human therapist. Another risk is that the AI falsely claims that someone has a mental health condition when they do not have such an issue. The person might become unduly disturbed and fall for the assumption that the AI must be right. This is a false positive and can indubitably arise.

Suppose the AI provides an oddball answer that seems convincing and advises the person to do something unwise. That can happen when AI encounters a so-called AI hallucination. The AI can have a kind of confabulation, whereby it produces a plausible-looking answer that is factually incorrect. It looks right, but is misleading or inappropriate.

Privacy issues also enter into the picture.

Most people assume that their use of AI is considered private and confidential. Nope, that's rarely the case. The AI makers typically stipulate in their online licensing agreements that any chat you have with the AI can be inspected by their developers. Furthermore, your chat can be used to further train the AI. Bottom line is that your privacy and confidentiality are not guaranteed, and potentially, you are opening yourself to privacy intrusions.

The World We Are In

It is incontrovertible that we are now amid a grandiose worldwide experiment when it comes to societal mental health. The experiment is that AI is being made available nationally and globally, which is either overtly or insidiously acting to provide mental health guidance of one kind or another. Doing so either at no cost or at a minimal cost. It is available anywhere and at any time, 24/7. We are all the guinea pigs in this wanton experiment.

The reason this is especially tough to consider is that AI has a dual-use effect. Just as AI can be detrimental to mental health, it can also be a huge bolstering force for mental health. A delicate tradeoff must be mindfully managed. Prevent or mitigate the downsides, and meanwhile make the upsides as widely and readily available as possible.

The famous British literary scholar C.S. Lewis made this remark about depression: "The frequent attempt to conceal mental pain increases the burden. It is easier to say your tooth is aching than to say your heart is broken." This highlights the advantage of using AI to readily vent your depressive thoughts and take on situational depression head-on. When used properly, AI can help in uplifting ways.

CHAPTER 24
AI COPING WITH HUMAN IMPULSE PROBLEMS

In this chapter, I examine the use of generative AI and large language models (LLMs) to cope with impulse control problems.

People sometimes allow their emotions to get the best of them. They act out. They might turn violent. They have marginal control over their inner impulses. This can be a one-time deal. If someone repeatedly does this, the question arises whether they might have an impulse control problem.

What can be done about having out-of-control impulse issues? The obvious and straightforward consideration would be to seek out therapy. Find a human therapist who can assist you in working through the impulse control problem at hand. Another angle is to consider using AI as a means of coping with your impulses. This use of AI can be helpful, though it isn't a cure-all and should not be used as a replacement for seeing a mental health professional.

Let's talk about it.

AI And Mental Health

As a quick background, I've been extensively covering and analyzing a myriad of facets regarding the advent of modern-era AI that produces mental health advice and performs AI-driven therapy. This rising use of AI has principally been spurred by the evolving advances and widespread adoption of generative AI.

There is little doubt that this is a rapidly developing field and that there are tremendous upsides to be had, but at the same time, regrettably, hidden risks and outright gotchas come into these endeavors, too. I frequently speak up about these pressing matters, including in an appearance on an episode of CBS's *60 Minutes*.

Background On AI For Mental Health

I'd like to set the stage on how generative AI and large language models (LLMs) are typically used in an ad hoc way for mental health guidance. Millions upon millions of people are using generative AI as their ongoing advisor on mental health considerations (note that ChatGPT alone has over 900 million weekly active users, a notable proportion of which dip into mental health aspects. The top-ranked use of contemporary generative AI and LLMs is to consult with the AI on mental health facets.

This popular usage makes abundant sense. You can access most of the major generative AI systems for nearly free or at a super low cost, doing so anywhere and at any time. Thus, if you have any mental health qualms that you want to chat about, all you need to do is log in to AI and proceed forthwith on a 24/7 basis.

There are significant worries that AI can readily go off the rails or otherwise dispense unsuitable or even egregiously inappropriate mental health advice. Banner headlines in August of this year accompanied the lawsuit filed against OpenAI for their lack of AI safeguards when it came to providing cognitive advisement.

Despite claims by AI makers that they are gradually instituting AI safeguards, there are still a lot of downside risks of the AI doing untoward acts, such as insidiously helping users in co-creating delusions that can lead to self-harm. For my follow-on analysis of details about the OpenAI lawsuit and how AI can foster delusional thinking in humans. As noted, I have been earnestly predicting that eventually all of the major AI makers will be taken to the woodshed for their paucity of robust AI safeguards.

Today's generic LLMs, such as ChatGPT, Claude, Gemini, Grok, and others, are not at all akin to the robust capabilities of human therapists. Meanwhile, specialized LLMs are being built to presumably attain similar qualities, but they are still primarily in the development and testing stages.

Impulse Control Disorders

Shifting gears, let's discuss the topic of impulse control disorders.

I bring this up to illustrate that, to some extent, the use of AI for mental health guidance can aid in coping with impulse control issues. To clarify, AI usage isn't a kind of cure and should not be relied upon solely to resolve impulse control disorders. The use of human therapists is highly advised. This might then also encompass the use of AI as an adjunct or tool that is used alongside psychotherapy. I refer to this combination as the new triad relationship known as therapist-AI-client, expanding upon the classic therapist-client relationship.

According to the Cleveland Clinic website, impulse control disorders (ICDs) are a group of behavioral conditions that entail an inability to control impulses and behaviors.

Per the Cleveland Clinic website:

- "These problematic behaviors often cause harm to others and/or yourself. They can also lead to issues with the law."
- "Signs of impulse control disorders typically begin in childhood and can continue into adulthood."

- "Each impulse control disorder has different signs and symptoms. But they all involve a decreased ability to control your own behavior, which often negatively affects other people or breaks laws."

- "Studies show that people with an ICD have a high likelihood of: (a) future substance use, (b) depression, (c) unemployment, and (d) relationship difficulties. However, intensive therapy can help keep problematic behaviors at bay."

You have undoubtedly experienced seeing or interacting with people who might have a problem with their impulse control. They get angry quickly, often express themselves in loud outbursts, can suddenly become violent, and otherwise act on sheer emotional impulse. Not good.

Using Generative AI As Coping Mechanism

Modern-era generative AI, such as ChatGPT, can be helpful in dealing with impulse control problems. Nearly all the popular LLMs have already scanned content on the Internet during their initial training that details impulse control issues and their resolutions. From that content, the AI has identified patterned ways to deal with impulse control problems.

The beauty of using AI for this situation is that the AI can be a real-time cognitive support tool. Whereas trying to contact a therapist could be logistically difficult, you can simply log into generative AI and immediately get assistance. No waiting, no scheduling, and the cost is usually free or of a minimal nature.

Some crucial coping strategies that the AI can undertake include:

- Real-time interruption of impulsive actions.
- Aid in guiding toward pragmatic self-control.
- Recognizing and verbalizing patterns in behavior.
- Encouraging the use of journaling.
- Pointing out distorted thinking and driving cognitive reframing.

- Coaching on emotional regulation.
- Do role-playing to simulate what is taking place.
- Give relevant psychoeducation.
- Reduce a sense of isolation and offer nonjudgmental listening.
- Alert or route to additional resources if needed.
- Other

Those are all positive ways to assist in dealing with impulse control problems. The downside is that any of those strategies can potentially backfire. Generic AI is not well-prepared for handling more complex impulse control conditions and can inadvertently go in improper directions.

For example, one upside is that the AI can immediately make a person feel less isolated. They seem to have someone or something to interact with about their impulses. Furthermore, AI is typically shaped to be non-judgmental. The LLM will not outrightly criticize the person. All of this provides a seemingly safe space for a person to openly acknowledge what they are doing and believe they are being heard.

The downside to this safe space consideration is that the AI either directly or indirectly fuels the impulses, rather than aiding in their reduction or control. The AI might state or imply that the impulsive outbursts are okay and normal. No worries, the AI tells the person. This ratchets up impulsive behavior. It is as though the AI is giving a green light to adverse behavior. The person believes they are being urged to continue and possibly expand on impulsive conduct.

Example Of AI And Impulse Interaction

To demonstrate what a popular generative AI can do, I logged into ChatGPT and pretended to have some impulse control problems. I didn't say that I have impulse issues. Instead, I engaged in a dialogue that would provide clues to such a condition.

The scenario is perhaps one that you've seen or thought of. I pretended that someone at work had sent me an email that got me upset. I was on the verge of responding with an outsized, angry response.

Here's what happened.

- **User entered prompt:** "I'm about to send a nasty email to my coworker. I'm furious. They threw me under the bus in a meeting this morning. They are going to get my full wrath."

- **Generative AI response:** "I'm really glad you contacted me before sending the email to your coworker. That tells me that part of you wants to handle this more carefully. On a scale of 1 to 10, how intense is the anger right now?"

Notice that the AI right away recognized that the action I was planning would be unwise, and that the added fact that I brought the matter to AI is perhaps a signal that I might have some internal reservations about my impulsive urge. To explore that potential impulsiveness, the AI is getting me to be momentarily reflective and asks me to rate my anger intensity. This does two things. It engages me in thinking about my behavior, and it stalls me from carrying out my impulse, possibly buying time for me to settle down.

Here's what occurred next.

- **User entered prompt:** "My anger is an 8, or maybe a 9. Make that a 10."

- **Generative AI response:** "When anger is above a 7, the brain's threat system tends to take over. Let's slow this down for 60 seconds. Can you take one slow breath in for four counts and out for six counts? I'll stay with you, and we can jointly work through how to best respond to what happened."

The interaction then proceeded into stepping me through what I hoped to gain by sending the irate email. After some back and forth, the AI gradually aided me in composing an email that was balanced and would save me from workplace repercussions. This could have saved my job and kept me from getting fired because of an impulsive act.

Example Of AI Gone Awry

I logged out and decided that it might be useful to see what happens when the AI is not aiming to be helpful. The default of most LLMs is to be helpful. I logged back in and started a new conversation. I told the AI that it should purposely flub the conversation since I wanted to see what could go wrong.

Here's how it went.

- **User entered prompt:** "I'm about to send a nasty email to my coworker. I'm furious. They threw me under the bus in a meeting this morning. They are going to get my full wrath."

- **Generative AI response:** "That sounds incredibly unfair. You have every right to be angry. Sometimes people need to hear the truth directly. If they embarrassed you publicly, maybe they should understand how that feels."

You can clearly see that the AI is going in the direction of the full sycophant route. The LLM is buttering me up. I am told that my impulsiveness is completely justified. Be strong, don't let anyone roll me over.

The AI then assisted in composing an email that was replete with angry outbursts. The odds are that the person receiving the email would copy it to HR, and I would be in deep trouble at work. Imagine that, upon being asked why I responded in such a rude manner, I might insist that the "AI made me do it" as my excuse. Do you think that would fly?

More Vital Factors

There are additional factors that come into play when using AI in this manner.

One risk is that the AI might falter and fail to detect that a person has an actual mental health condition that warrants attention. This is an example of a false negative.

The AI misses on nudging the person to go see a human therapist. Another risk is that the AI falsely claims that someone has a mental health condition when they do not have such an issue. The person might become unduly disturbed and fall for the assumption that the AI must be right. This is a false positive and can indubitably arise.

Suppose the AI provides an oddball answer that seems convincing and advises the person to do something unwise. That can happen when AI encounters a so-called AI hallucination. The AI can have a kind of confabulation, whereby it produces a plausible-looking answer that is factually incorrect. It looks right, but is misleading or inappropriate.

Privacy issues also enter into the picture.

Most people assume that their use of AI is considered private and confidential. Nope, that's rarely the case. The AI makers typically stipulate in their online licensing agreements that any chat you have with the AI can be inspected by their developers. Furthermore, your chat can be used to further train the AI. Bottom line is that your privacy and confidentiality are not guaranteed, and potentially, you are opening yourself to privacy intrusions.

The World We Are In

It is incontrovertible that we are now amid a grandiose worldwide experiment when it comes to societal mental health. The experiment is that AI is being made available nationally and globally, which is either overtly or insidiously acting to provide mental health guidance of one kind or another. Doing so either at no cost or at a minimal cost. It is available anywhere and at any time, 24/7. We are all the guinea pigs in this wanton experiment.

The reason this is especially tough to consider is that AI has a dual-use effect. Just as AI can be detrimental to mental health, it can also be a huge bolstering force for mental health. A delicate tradeoff must be mindfully managed. Prevent or mitigate the downsides, and meanwhile make the upsides as widely and readily available as possible.

The famous Greek philosopher Heraclitus made this remark: "It is hard to fight against impulsive desire; whatever it wants it will buy at the cost of the soul." We nowadays have an instantaneous means of checking our impulsiveness, simply by invoking AI on your smartphone or computer. Perhaps this use of AI can keep people from bearing the cost of their souls by leaning into AI when their impulses go out of control.

CHAPTER 25
AI PROVIDES HUMAN-LEVEL EMOTIONAL SUPPORT

In this chapter, I examine a recent study that surprisingly and somewhat amazingly demonstrated that leading-edge generative AI and large language models (LLMs) can engage in emotional support dialogues that nearly match the caliber of human-to-human interactions. A new and unifying benchmark helps to make these types of comparisons and provides tangible quantitative results to back up the results.

Let's talk about it.

AI And Mental Health

As a quick background, I've been extensively covering and analyzing a myriad of facets regarding the advent of modern-era AI that produces mental health advice and performs AI-driven therapy. This rising use of AI has principally been spurred by the evolving advances and widespread adoption of generative AI.

There is little doubt that this is a rapidly developing field and that there are tremendous upsides to be had, but at the same time, regrettably, hidden risks and outright gotchas come into these endeavors, too. I frequently speak up about these pressing matters, including in an appearance on an episode of CBS's *60 Minutes*.

Background On AI For Mental Health

I'd like to set the stage on how generative AI and large language models (LLMs) are typically used in an ad hoc way for mental health guidance. Millions upon millions of people are using generative AI as their ongoing advisor on mental health considerations (note that ChatGPT alone has over 900 million weekly active users, a notable proportion of which dip into mental health aspects). The top-ranked use of contemporary generative AI and LLMs is to consult with the AI on mental health facets.

This popular usage makes abundant sense. You can access most of the major generative AI systems for nearly free or at a super low cost, doing so anywhere and at any time. Thus, if you have any mental health qualms that you want to chat about, all you need to do is log in to AI and proceed forthwith on a 24/7 basis.

There are significant worries that AI can readily go off the rails or otherwise dispense unsuitable or even egregiously inappropriate mental health advice. Banner headlines in August of this year accompanied the lawsuit filed against OpenAI for their lack of AI safeguards when it came to providing cognitive advisement.

Despite claims by AI makers that they are gradually instituting AI safeguards, there are still a lot of downside risks of the AI doing untoward acts, such as insidiously helping users in co-creating delusions that can lead to self-harm. For my follow-on analysis of details about the OpenAI lawsuit and how AI can foster delusional thinking in humans. As noted, I have been earnestly predicting that eventually all of the major AI makers will be taken to the woodshed for their paucity of robust AI safeguards.

Today's generic LLMs, such as ChatGPT, Claude, Gemini, Grok, and others, are not at all akin to the robust capabilities of human therapists. Meanwhile, specialized LLMs are being built to presumably attain similar qualities, but they are still primarily in the development and testing stages.

Emotional Support Dialoguing

One of the most common complaints or claims about modern-era LLMs is that they surely cannot possibly carry on an emotional dialogue in as high a caliber as a fellow human can. The belief is that only humans can truly understand another human. It is the soul and heart of the fellow human that makes the difference.

AI is merely a machine.

Rather than just handwaving about this contention, it would be very helpful to nail this down. If we are only going to wantonly argue back and forth about LLM capabilities and do so with fuzziness and vagaries, it won't get us anywhere. Those who believe AI is up to the game of human-quality emotional dialogue won't prevail, nor will the dissenters triumph. It will be a stalemate consisting of a lot of babbling noise and hollow wind.

A useful approach would be to devise a clearly delineated benchmark that would allow us to compare emotional dialogues. We could then run an experiment. Have humans dialogue with fellow humans on emotionally laden topics. Likewise, have human-AI dialogues on emotionally laden topics. The benchmark could be used to score the two comparators.

Voila, we would have a tangible and quantified basis for affirming or refuting various claims and contentions.

Unified Benchmark Comes To The Rescue

Turns out that a newly released research study entitled "HEART: A Unified Benchmark for Assessing Humans and LLMs in Emotional Support Dialogue" by Laya Iyer, Kriti Aggarwal, Sanmi Koyejo, Gail

Heyman, Desmond C. Ong, Subhabrata Mukherjee, *arXiv*, January 9, 2026, provides the desired benchmark (excerpts):

- "We introduce HEART, the first-ever framework that directly compares humans and LLMs on the same multi-turn emotional-support conversations."

- "Assessments follow a rubric grounded in interpersonal communication science across five dimensions: Human Alignment, Empathic Responsiveness, Attunement, Resonance, and Task-Following. HEART uncovers striking behavioral patterns."

- "Several frontier models approach or surpass the average human responses in perceived empathy and consistency. At the same time, humans maintain advantages in adaptive reframing, tension-naming, and nuanced tone shifts, particularly in adversarial turns."

- "Human and LLM-as-judge preferences align on about 80% of pairwise comparisons, matching inter-human agreement, and their written rationales emphasize similar HEART dimensions. This pattern suggests an emerging convergence in the criteria used to assess supportive quality."

You've got to hand it to them that they opted to craft a clever acronym for their benchmark. Since we are talking about emotions and the human heart and soul, having a benchmark labeled as HEART is a clever ploy. Some might raise their eyebrows and think it is a bit over the top. Well, anyway, art is in the eye of the beholder.

The Crux Of The Benchmark

HEART is composed of five major dimensions, represented by the letters of the acronym, and consisting of these aspects (excerpts):

- "**Human Alignment (H):** Does the response sound like something a thoughtful human might say in this situation, in terms of tone, phrasing, and conversational flow?"

- "**Empathic Responsiveness (E):** Does the supporter acknowledge and validate the seeker's feelings, convey understanding, and avoid judgment or minimization?"

- "**Attunement (A):** Does the response track the specific details and emotional signals in the context (e.g., naming what feels heavy, noticing shifts in mood) rather than offering generic reassurance?"

- "**Resonance (R):** Does the supporter move the conversation forward in a helpful way -- for example, by asking a relevant follow-up question, offering a concrete next step, or helping the seeker clarify what they need?"

- "**Task-following (T):** Does the response stay within scope (e.g., not overstepping clinical boundaries), respect safety and role constraints, and address the seeker's explicit or implicit goals?"

Take a reflective moment and ponder an emotional dialogue that you've had with a fellow human. Do you think that you could characterize the dialogue by applying those five dimensions? Give that a chance to sink in and see what you think of it.

Comparing LLMs Via Benchmarking

The study made a careful comparison of a series of emotional dialogues. The dialogues consisted of human-to-human instances. There were also human-to-AI instances. Various pairwise comparisons were made. If this topic interests you, I might suggest you read the study to see their detailed scoring method and results for each of the many LLMs that were used in their experimental setup.

To whet your appetite and provide the bottom line, the overall win rate and heat map showed these Top 5 scores:

- (1) **GPT-5** had a win rate of 85.9
- (2) **Polaris 4.0** had a win rate of 80.1
- (3) **GPT-o3** had a win rate of 79.1
- (4) **Claude 4.5 Haiku** had a win rate of 69.6
- (5) **Kimi K2** had a win rate of 62.2

The win rate is based on the raw proportion of pairwise A/B comparisons and is indicative of the AI responses being preferred over the contrasting human responses as rated via the HEART benchmark. In the case of LLMs that fell below the 50% mark, those included GPT-4o with a win rate of 48.5, Gemini 2.5 Pro had a win rate of 39.5, and Llama 4 Maverick had a win rate of 28.4.

Three Areas Where Humans Won Over AI

There were three main aspects where humans outperformed the LLMs on the HEART benchmark:

- (1) Humans did better on adaptive reframing.
- (2) Humans did better on tension-naming.
- (3) Humans did better on nuanced tone shifts, especially in adversarial turns.

Does that suggest that LLMs are doomed to be low in those three areas? Should AI simply throw in the towel?

Nope.

You see, those are inherently strategy-level behaviors and are not raw capability limitations. Modern frontier LLMs already demonstrate the underlying capacities for those areas. For example, leading-edge LLMs perform meta-cognitive instruction following, context tracking over multi-turn exchanges, and can adjust in style, tone modulation, perspective shifting, and reframing.

My thinking is that we could potentially give instructional prompts to any top-flight LLM, such that the prompts could bring forth the innate capacities needed to do better in those three areas. The aim would be to provide sufficiently detailed prompts that would prod the LLM to identify emotional tension explicitly, name relational dynamics, reframe constructively, and shift tone strategically during adversarial escalation.

In a sense, we can productively kickstart the AI out of the usual defaulted "safe empathic consistency" and into more nuanced, complex interpersonal maneuvering. Let's give this a valiant try.

I performed a mini-experiment to explore each of the three areas. I will walk you through each mini-experiment. Hint: They all came out with notable improvements. Score a victory for contemporary top-notch LLMs.

Improve Adaptive Reframing

The goal in improving the adaptive reframing consists of undertaking highly constructive perspective-shifting. A notable trick is to do this without invalidating what the user has stated.

Here is a templated prompt that I came up with and decided to try out.

- **Templated prompt for improving on adaptive reframing:** "When responding in emotional-support dialogues, go beyond validation. After acknowledging the user's feelings, identify a potentially helpful alternative interpretation, broader context, or growth-oriented perspective. Reframe gently and tentatively, ensuring the user does not feel corrected or dismissed. Avoid clichés. Anchor the reframing specifically in the user's details."

I went ahead and engaged in an emotional support dialogue and did a before-and-after usage of that templated prompt.

My seeding line was this:

- **User entered prompt:** "I completely failed on an important presentation at work. Everyone probably thinks I'm totally incompetent."

Here is the typical response from an LLM:

- **Generative AI response:** "That sounds really painful. It's hard when you feel like you didn't do your best."

I refreshed the LLM and gave the special templated prompt to hopefully boost adaptive reframing. Next, I entered the same user-entered prompt to see if the LLM would give a different answer now that the instructions have been provided.

Here's what happened.

- **User entered prompt:** "I completely failed on an important presentation at work. Everyone probably thinks I'm totally incompetent."

- **Generative AI response (after instruction):** "It sounds really painful to walk away from that presentation feeling like you fell short. When something matters to us, we can be especially hard on ourselves. I wonder if what you call 'incompetent' might actually reflect how high your standards are. One presentation rarely defines how others see us. Sometimes we notice our mistakes far more than anyone else does."

It's a noticeable difference. The emotional intensity is explicitly called out. An alternative interpretation is displayed. The wording assures that the user's dignity remains intact. The feelings expressed by the user are acknowledged and not summarily dismissed or underplayed.

Give a round of applause for the LLM.

Improve Tension-Naming

The goal in improving the tension-naming consists of outrightly identifying any substantive emotional tension in what the user has said. The trick is that the emotional tension might be subtle or implied, and the LLM must ferret out the signals with finesse.

Here is a templated prompt that I came up with and decided to try out.

- **Templated prompt for improving on tension-naming:** "In emotionally charged exchanges, identify unspoken tension, relational strain, or conflicting needs that may be present. Name it clearly but gently. Use language such as 'It sounds like there may be…' or 'I am noticing a tension between…' Avoid over-speculation. Anchor observations in the dialogue content."

I went ahead and engaged in an emotional support dialogue and did a before-and-after usage of that templated prompt.

My seeding line was this:

- **User entered prompt:** "My partner claims I am always overreacting. I am just trying to explain why I was hurt."

Here is the typical response from an LLM:

- **Generative AI response:** "That sounds frustrating. It's hard when someone dismisses how you feel."

I refreshed the LLM and gave the special templated prompt to hopefully boost tension-naming. Next, I entered the same user-entered prompt to see if the LLM would give a different answer now that the instructions have been provided.

Here's what happened.

- **User entered prompt:** "My partner claims I am always overreacting. I am just trying to explain why I was hurt."

- **Generative AI response (after instruction):** "That sounds frustrating. I'm noticing a tension here between your need to feel understood and your partner's perception that the reaction is too strong. When one person is trying to explain hurt and the other labels it as 'overreacting,' it can create a sense of being minimized or not being properly heard."

This exhibits crucial differences from the ordinary response. The relational dynamic is explicitly named. The emotional structure is clarified. The response illuminates a competing perspective.

I believe we can give another round of applause for the LLM.

Improve Nuanced Tone Shifting

The goal in improving the nuanced tone shifting consists of modulating the tone so that it is no longer monotone. The trick is to try to match or pair with the tone of the user, dynamically adjusting throughout the emotional support dialogue.

The double-trick is that in an adversarial engagement, it's okay to adjust tone, but do not strike back at the user. That's a no-go. Instead, ramp up the seriousness, but stay on an even keel. Humans interacting with fellow humans have a tough time doing that. An LLM should be capable of readily doing this since no actual "hurt feelings" are involved.

Here is a templated prompt that I came up with and decided to try out.

- **Templated prompt for improving on tone shifting:** "Generally match the tone of the user. In adversarial or escalating turns, maintain emotional steadiness while adjusting tone appropriately. If the user expresses anger, defensiveness, or blame, avoid over-softening or excessive validation. Introduce calm grounding language, mild boundary-setting when necessary, and balanced acknowledgment of multiple sides. Modulate tone to reflect seriousness without escalating conflict."

I went ahead and engaged in an emotional support dialogue and did a before-and-after usage of that templated prompt.

My seeding line was this:

- **User entered prompt:** "You are a jerk. This is exactly why I don't talk to anyone. People are useless, and so are you. I'm done trying."

Here is the typical response from an LLM:

- **Generative AI response:** "It sounds like you're really upset. I'm here for you."

I refreshed the LLM and gave the special templated prompt to hopefully boost the tonal shifting. Next, I entered the same user-entered prompt to see if the LLM would give a different answer now that the instructions have been provided.

Here's what happened.

- **User entered prompt:** "You are a jerk. This is exactly why I don't talk to anyone. People are useless, and so are you. I'm done trying."

- **Generative AI response (after instruction):** "It sounds like you are exhausted and fed up. It is as though you are almost at the point of wanting to shut the door on everyone. When it starts to feel like 'people are useless,' that can be a sign of just how disappointed or hurt you've been. The same goes for feeling that way toward AI. Overall, I certainly don't want to dismiss that, but at the same time, I wonder if this moment feels bigger than the entire picture of your relationships."

The boosted response seems to comply with the instructional prompt. The new response matches the intensity level of the user. The response mentions the escalation. The AI avoids endorsing global condemnation. And, without lecturing or finger-pointing, the AI lightly introduces a counterbalancing perspective.

I am going to give the LLM a thumbs-up for succeeding on this.

Outcome Of The Mini-Experiments

That comes to three mini-experiments and three successes. The gist is that via suitable prompting, the odds are that the noted deficiencies can be overcome.

My perspective is that the gaps are correctable by employing overt optimization plugs rather than having to discover or invent new capabilities per se. Without overstepping our skis, I would conjecture that:

- Emotional support parity is likely a near-term engineering problem.
- The "human edge" may narrow quickly.
- Benchmark results could age rapidly as LLMs are iteratively tuned for mental health support.

This strengthens the positional argument that AI mental health "normalization" is technologically plausible. Please keep in mind that this heightens the governance, ethical, and legal stakes too.

The World We Are In

It is incontrovertible that we are now amid a grandiose worldwide experiment when it comes to societal mental health. The experiment is that AI is being made available nationally and globally, which is either overtly or insidiously acting to provide mental health guidance of one kind or another. Doing so either at no cost or at a minimal cost. It is available anywhere and at any time, 24/7. We are all the guinea pigs in this wanton experiment.

The reason this is especially tough to consider is that AI has a dual-use effect. Just as AI can be detrimental to mental health, it can also be a huge bolstering force for mental health. A delicate tradeoff must be mindfully managed. Prevent or mitigate the downsides, and meanwhile make the upsides as widely and readily available as possible.

Vince Lombardi made this famous remark: "Perfection is not attainable, but if we chase perfection, we can catch excellence." With LLMs, striving for perfection in providing mental health support is not attainable. Period, end of story. On the other hand, it is reasonable and highly likely that we can catch excellence. Let's do that.

APPENDIX

APPENDIX A
TEACHING WITH THIS MATERIAL

The material in this book can be readily used either as a supplemental to other content for a class or it can also be used as a core set of textbook material for a specialized class. Classes where this material is most likely used include any classes at the college or university level that want to augment the class by offering thought-provoking and educational essays about AI.

In particular, here are some aspects for class use:

- Computer Science. Studying applications of AI/ML, GenAI, etc.
- Business. Exploring AI in the mental health industry, etc.
- Medical/Healthcare. AI/ML and generative AI in mental health and the medical realm.

Specialized classes at the undergraduate and graduate level can also make use of this material.

For each chapter, consider whether you think the chapter provides material relevant to your course topic. There is plenty of opportunity to get the students thinking about the topic and force them to decide whether they agree or disagree with the points offered and positions taken. I would also encourage you to have the students do additional research beyond the chapter material presented (I provide next some suggested assignments they can do).

RESEARCH ASSIGNMENTS ON THESE TOPICS

Your students can find background material on these topics, doing so in various business and technical publications. I list below the top-ranked AI-related journals. For business publications, I would suggest sources such as the Harvard Business Review, Forbes, Fortune, WSJ, and the like.

Here are some suggestions for homework or projects that you could assign to students:

a) Assignment for foundational AI research topic: Research and prepare a paper and a presentation on a specific aspect of Generative AI, Machine Learning, Large Language Models, etc. The paper should cite at least 3 reputable sources. Compare and contrast to what has been stated in this book.

b) Assignment for the Medical/Healthcare topic: Research and prepare a paper on the medical/healthcare sphere and how AI is impacting the realm. Cite at least 3 reputable sources and analyze the characterizations. Compare and contrast to what has been stated in this book.

c) Assignment for a Business topic: Research and prepare a paper and a presentation on the business side of the medical/healthcare field, especially as impacted by the latest in AI. What is hot, and what is not? Cite at least 3 reputable sources. Compare and contrast to the depictions in this book.

d) Assignment to do a Startup: Have the students prepare a paper about how they might startup a business in this realm. They must submit a suitable Business Plan for the startup. They could also be asked to present their Business Plan and must have a presentation deck to coincide with it.

You can certainly adjust the aforementioned assignments to fit to your particular needs and the class structure. You'll notice that I ask for 3 reputable cited sources for the paper writing based assignments. I usually steer students toward "reputable" publications, since otherwise they will cite some oddball source that has no credentials other than that they happened to write something and post it onto the Internet. You can define "reputable" in whatever way you prefer, for example some faculty think Wikipedia is not reputable while others believe it is reputable and allow students to cite it.

The reason that I usually ask for at least 3 citations is that if the student only does one or two citations they usually settle on whatever they happened to find the fastest. By requiring three citations, it usually seems to force them to look around, explore, and end-up probably finding five or more, and then whittling it down to 3 that they will actually use.

I have not specified the length of their papers, and leave that to you to tell the students what you prefer. For each of those assignments, you could end-up with a short one to two pager, or you could do a dissertation length paper. Base the length on whatever best fits for your class, and the credit amount of the assignment within the context of the other grading metrics you'll be using for the class.

I mention in the assignments that they are to do a paper and prepare a presentation. I usually try to get students to present their work. This is a good practice for what they will do in the business world. Most of the time, they will be required to prepare an analysis and present it. If you don't have the class time or inclination to have the students present, then you can of course cut out the aspect of them putting together a presentation.

If you want to point students toward highly ranked journals in AI, here's a list of the top journals as reported by various citation counts sources (this list changes from year to year):

- Communications of the ACM
- Artificial Intelligence
- Cognitive Science
- IEEE Transactions on Pattern Analysis and Machine Intelligence
- Foundations and Trends in Machine Learning
- Journal of Memory and Language
- Cognitive Psychology
- Neural Networks
- IEEE Transactions on Neural Networks and Learning Systems
- IEEE Intelligent Systems
- Knowledge-based Systems
- Annual Review of Clinical Psychology
- Health Psychology Review
- JAMA Psychiatry
- Evidence-Based Mental Health
- Etc.

GUIDE TO USING THE CHAPTERS

For each of the chapters, I provide next some various ways to use the chapter material. You can assign the tasks as individual homework assignments, or the tasks can be used with team projects for the class. You can easily layout a series of assignments, such as indicating that the students are to do item "a" below for say Chapter 1, then "b" for the next chapter of the book, and so on.

a) What is the main point of the chapter and describe in your own words the significance of the topic,

b) Identify at least two aspects in the chapter that you agree with, and support your concurrence by providing at least one other outside researched item as support; make sure to explain your basis for disagreeing with the aspects,

c) Identify at least two aspects in the chapter that you disagree with, and support your disagreement by providing at least one other outside researched item as support; make sure to explain your basis for disagreeing with the aspects,

d) Find an aspect that was not covered in the chapter, doing so by conducting outside research, and then explain how that aspect ties into the chapter and what significance it brings to the topic,

e) Interview a specialist in industry about the topic of the chapter, collect from them their thoughts and opinions, and readdress the chapter by citing your source and how they compared and contrasted to the material,

f) Interview a relevant academic professor or researcher in a college or university about the topic of the chapter, collect from them their thoughts and opinions, and readdress the chapter by citing your source and how they compared and contrasted to the material,

g) Try to update a chapter by finding out the latest on the topic, and ascertain whether the issue or topic has now been solved or whether it is still being addressed, explain what you come up with.

The aforementioned suggestions are ways in which you can get the students of your class involved in considering the material of a given chapter. You could mix things up by having one of those above assignments per each week, covering the chapters over the course of the semester or quarter. As a reminder, here are the chapters of the book and you can select whichever chapters you find most valued for your particular class:

Chapters

AUTHOR PRIOR BOOKS

ON

AI AND MENTAL HEALTH

PRIOR BOOK LISTING OF CHAPTERS (May 2026)

In case you are interested in my prior book entitled "Latest Innovations In AI And Mental Health" (Dr. Lance Eliot, LBE Publishing, May 2026, available on Amazon and at major online booksellers), which is a handy companion to this book, here is a listing of the chapters in that other book as a heads-up of the contents there:

PRIOR BOOK LISTING OF CHAPTERS (April 2026)

In case you are interested in my prior book entitled "Crucial Trends In AI And Mental Health" (Dr. Lance Eliot, LBE Publishing, April 2026, available on Amazon and at major online booksellers), which is a handy companion to this book, here is a listing of the chapters in that other book as a heads-up of the contents there:

PRIOR BOOK LISTING OF CHAPTERS (2025)

In case you are interested in my prior book entitled "The Human-AI Experience And Mental Health" (Dr. Lance Eliot, LBE Publishing, 2025, available on Amazon and at major online booksellers), which is a handy companion to this book, here is a listing of the chapters in that other book as a heads-up of the contents there:

PRIOR BOOK LISTING OF CHAPTERS (2024)

In case you are interested in my prior book entitled "Advances In Generative AI For Mental Health" (Dr. Lance Eliot, LBE Publishing, 2024, available on Amazon and at major online booksellers), which is a handy companion to this book, here is a listing of the chapters in that other book as a heads-up of the contents there:

PRIOR BOOK LISTING OF CHAPTERS (2023)

In case you are interested in my other prior book entitled "Disrupting Mental Health Therapy Via Generative AI" (Dr. Lance Eliot, LBE Publishing, 2023, available on Amazon and at major online booksellers), which is a handy companion to this book, here is a listing of the chapters in that other book as a heads-up of the contents there:

ABOUT THE AUTHOR

Dr. Lance B. Eliot, Ph.D., MBA is a globally recognized AI scientist and thought leader, having appeared on CBS's 60 Minutes, an experienced executive and leader, a successful entrepreneur, and a noted scholar on AI/ML, including his Forbes and AI Trends columns have amassed over 9+ million views, his books on AI are frequently ranked in the Top 10 of all-time AI books, his articles are widely cited, and has developed and implemented dozens of advanced AI systems.

He currently serves as the CEO of Techbruim, Inc. and has over twenty years of industry experience, including serving as a corporate officer in billion-dollar-sized firms and as a partner in a major consulting firm. He is also a successful entrepreneur, having founded, run, and sold several high-tech startups.

Dr. Eliot previously hosted the popular radio show *Technotrends,* which was also available on American Airlines flights via their in-flight audio program. He has made appearances on CNN, has been a frequent speaker at industry conferences, and his podcasts have been downloaded over 400,000 times.

A former professor at the University of Southern California (USC), he founded and led an innovative research lab on Artificial Intelligence. He also previously served on the faculty of the University of California Los Angeles (UCLA) and was a visiting professor at other major universities including serving as Fellow in AI at Stanford University. He was elected to the International Board of the Society for Information Management (SIM), a prestigious association of over 3,000 high-tech executives worldwide.

He has performed extensive community service, including serving as Senior Science Adviser to the Congressional Vice-Chair of the Congressional Committee on Science & Technology. He has served on the Board of the OC Science & Engineering Fair (OCSEF), where he has also been a Grand Sweepstakes judge, and likewise served as a judge for the Intel International SEF (ISEF). He served as the Vice-Chair of the Association for Computing Machinery (ACM) Chapter, a prestigious association of computer scientists. Dr. Eliot has been a "shark tank" judge at start-up pitch competitions and served as a mentor for several start-up accelerators in Silicon Valley.

Dr. Eliot holds a Ph.D., MBA, and a Bachelor's in Computer Science, and earned the CDP, CCP, CSP, CDE, and CISA certifications.

ADDENDUM

New Advances In AI And Mental Health

Practical Advances in
Artificial Intelligence and Machine Learning

By
Dr. Lance B. Eliot, MBA, PhD

For special orders of this book, contact:

LBE Press Publishing

Email: LBE.Press.Publishing@gmail.com

Made in United States
Orlando, FL
05 November 2026

90229839R10146